Contents

Advent & Christmas

Lent, Triduum, & Easter

Ordinary Time

Guided Meditations for Teens

Living through the Church Year

Sydney Ann Merritt

Resource Publications, Inc.
San Jose, California

Reprint Department
Resource Publications, Inc.
160 E. Virginia Street #290
San Jose, CA 95112-5876
1-408-286-8505 (voice)
1-408-287-8748 (fax)

Library of Congress Cataloging in Publication Data
Merritt, Sydney Ann.
    Guided meditations for teens : living through the church year / Sydney Ann Merritt.
        p.   cm.
    Includes bibliographical references and index.
    ISBN 0-89390-402-3
    1. Church group work with teenagers. 2. Teenagers—
Prayer books and devotions—English. 3. Meditation—Christianity.
4. Church year meditations. I. Title.
    BV4447.M47   1997
    259'.23—dc21   97-33508

Printed in the United States of America

01 00 99 98 97 | 5 4 3 2 1

Editorial director: Nick Wagner
Prepress manager: Elizabeth J. Asborno
Cover design: Alan Villatuya, Mike Sagara
Production assistant: David Dunlap

To Thomas
of St.Christopher Church, San Jose, California,
a teen who touched my heart
with the love of God.
Bless you, always.

Acknowledgments

Love and gratitude to my husband, Lee, who has spent a lifetime sharing me with children, art, grandchildren, and my writing. He has given me the quiet strength and encouragement to be independent. He has never told me, "You can't get there from here," the greatest gift of all.

Teaching Young Adults to Experience Jesus through Prayer

The meditations presented in this book are an effective method of helping young adults learn how to experience Jesus within themselves—in their minds and hearts. The meditations follow the church seasons and are based on the lectionary Gospel readings for cycles A, B, and C. At the beginning of each meditation, I list the related Scripture citation, Sunday and season (with cycle[s] indicated in parentheses), and suggested background music.

The book speaks to the spiritual lives of teens, helping them to establish a place in their imaginations where they can be with Jesus. Our teenagers have been raised on instant popcorn, instant coffee, and instant entertainment on the TV set. Where, then, does that leave the concept of prayer? It may not be happening except for a quick, "Get me through this, Lord!" Reading the Bible, God's word, falls into an even more difficult category: unless it can be shown in "instant replay," the chances are that it is seldom, if ever, opened.

Meditations will reawaken the young people's imagination, as in the days of their childhood when play was their main activity. The meditations are designed to meet an uncomplicated and direct way of understanding the word of God. The teens are led into a Gospel scene where they will encounter the Lord through touch, feel, love, and prayer. The pages of the Bible will become alive when they "hear" the brush of angels' wings, experience the healing touch of Jesus at the tomb of Lazarus, and feel the force of wild hurricane winds as they cross the Sea of Galilee with Jesus.

The meditations can be merged into any catechetical program. For those who use CELEBRATING THE LECTIONARY from Resource Publications, Inc., you can incorporate the meditations into your weekly lesson plans as an alternate activity or use them as introductions or conclusions to a unit.

The introductions to many of the meditations relate my personal anecdotes or feelings and reflections. You may choose to read the introductions as written, explaining that they come from the writer's perspective, or you may adapt them to fit your own experiences or situations. The introductions are meant only as a starting point for the meditations.

Group discussion questions follow each meditation. I recommend small groups of four to six young people rather than sharing in a large group. For one thing, it is less intimidating. A teen may feel more comfortable sharing with three others than with a roomful of people. Working within a small group also allows more time for discussion. I have indicated times when you may prefer general discussion. I do not suggest inviting the teens to share their own experience of the meditation because this should remain a personal time with Jesus. However, if a teen volunteers to share his/her experiences, you will find that it stimulates the discussion time. Activities and closing prayer services are also included with most meditations.

Suggestions for Success

Sharing the experience of Jesus through prayer should be rewarding spiritually for the presenter as well as for the students. Following a few simple suggestions will help to insure your success.

To Begin

Begin with "A Place to Meet," the introductory guided meditation found at the end of this introduction. This will create a place in the young person's imagination to meet Jesus.

Personal Reflection

Before presenting a meditation, take a few minutes for your personal reflection on the Gospel scene. What images quicken your imagination? Ask yourself, "What is Jesus saying to me?"

Practice

To help you become more comfortable with this form of prayer, practice reading the meditation aloud slowly just as you will with the group. You may choose to record and play back the meditation, listening for pauses and voice inflection. Are you speaking too softly or too quickly? Are you pausing long enough?

- Read slowly with slight pauses where indicated (....). For longer pauses, wait sixty seconds or until you notice the teens becoming restless.

- Avoid speaking in a monotone. Change your voice to emphasize a change in character or scene.

Music

Background music is very important; it sets the tone and helps activate the imagination. You will find music suggestions at the beginning of each meditation. (See "Music Resources" for the listing of suggested recorded music.) For teens, music is an important part of their lives. I have found that in working with teens, it is much better to offer background music which includes sounds of nature—wind, rain, the sea, etc.—rather than traditional forms of music. Live music and sounds—soft guitar strumming, gentle piano music, tinkling wind chimes—can also be helpful.

Space

Give some thought to how you will create an atmosphere of prayer for the young people.

- Lower the lights or pull the shades.
- Use a candle.
- When possible, teens like being outdoors, stretched out on the grass, enjoying the touch of nature.
- Create a focal point by combining important elements: an open Bible; a candle; natural objects like rocks, driftwood, or greenery; other items of significance to the teens.

Make sure the students will be physically comfortable. Is the room too hot or too cold? Some may prefer sitting in their own seat or sitting on the floor rather than lying on the floor. Floor pillows are a great way of indicating private space.

Discussion

Allow time for discussion questions. Invite responses, but do not demand participation. Stress that in most cases there is no wrong or right answer; the answer is based on how they "feel" about a subject or how they imagine the outcome. Introspective questions should be done in a small group or during the prayer time. Gradually, teens will learn to trust themselves and earn the trust of others in their small groups.

Keep Trying

Do not become discouraged if your first attempts are not what you hoped for. Even your first awkward attempts will have an impact. Each young person will take home something different after his/her visit with Jesus. Believe it or not, teenagers will actually enjoy the quiet and calm of meditation.

The Meeting Place

Suggested Music: *The Sea*

Sometimes we allow ourselves to become so busy that we do not take time to listen for the voice of God in our lives. Often the day becomes a whirlwind of activity and people. "Where do I fit God into my schedule?" we wonder. Life seems to go much better when we take the time to say, "Good morning, Jesus," as we wake and to give thanks at the end of our days. In the quiet of your day, wait in silence for the voice of your Lord.

Would it be easier for you to communicate with Jesus if you could see him? Why?

There is a way we can see Jesus. It is called our imagination. You remember playing policeman, cowboy, or teacher, don't you? The same tool you used then to talk the talk and make the noises is still with you; your imagination is alive and well.

If you could use your imagination to go any place you wanted right now, where would that be? Given a choice, where would you want to meet Jesus? (*Invite discussion.*) Let's try taking a journey into our imaginations.

Remind the group that this is their private time to talk to Jesus and to listen to his voice within their hearts. Even though they are young adults you may need to remind them to not disturb the others with comments or noise. If you have a group that you know to be disruptive, separate them before you begin the meditation. Don't forget, the music choice can make or break the experience.

5

Meditation

Find a comfortable position....Close your eyes....Shrug your shoulders....Relax your muscles....Allow yourself to drift into the soft music....Take a deep breath....Let out it slowly.... Whisper, "Jesus."....

Imagine that you are walking down a winding path on a warm spring day....The blue-green sea caresses the sandy beach.... Waves pound the distant shoreline, sending white, foamy sprays of water high into the air....Sea gulls signal the return of the fishing boats....A tall man with long flowing hair stands in the middle of the pathway....He smiles as though he knows you....Can you see him?....He calls you by name....It is Jesus!...."Where are you going, Lord?" you ask....Jesus smiles, "Any place your imagination can take me."....He grasps your hand with a firm handshake...."Come and follow," he responds....You and Jesus walk side by side down the sloping hillside to water's edge....Jesus lowers himself to the ground, resting his back against a tamarind tree....Study his face....Does he look the way you have always pictured him?.... Grasping a small stone, he throws it into the waiting water. The rock skips, picking and choosing its path....Jesus dips his hand into the cool water, forms a cup with his hand, then offers you a drink....The water is cold. The summer sun has not yet warmed the tide....Jesus dips his hand into the water once again....Playfully, he splashes cold droplets of water on your bare legs....Put your hand into the water....Push the water with the palm of your hand....A cool spray washes over Jesus....You and Jesus laugh....

Taking Jesus by the arm, lead him to your favorite place....

Tall trees line the path, stretching their branches in salute to the heavens....The air smells of fresh, sweet grass and wildflowers....Look up at the sky....Clouds slowly drift across the face of the sun....A gust of warm air tugs at your hair.... You are now at your special place....It may be at home, a park, high in the mountains, or on a long sandy beach....You can be with Jesus wherever you want to be....Invite Jesus to sit down....No one knows that you are here....This is your time and place to be with Jesus....Feel the safety of his presence.... Feel his love....You are alone with Jesus in your favorite place.

I will give you a few moments to be alone with Jesus....Speak to him quietly in your heart....Ask him anything you want.... Talk to him....Share the things that weigh heavily upon your mind....(*Pause until the teens become restless.*) Look up into Jesus' face....His eyes look beyond your being, for he has walked with God....Listen to his voice....

Prayer

Jesus, I have often failed to take the time to talk with you. My days are filled with people and problems.
Help me to be more aware of your presence in my life.
I offer my words of thanks and praise. Steady my walk with you. Amen.

It is time for you to leave....Jesus wraps his arms around you and gives you a warm hug...."Goodbye for now," he says.... Turn and walk away....Wave goodbye....Open your eyes and return to this room.

Part I

Advent
&
Christmas

Prepare the Way for Your Lord

Scripture: Mt 3:1-12; Mk 13:33-37
Feast: First Sunday of Advent (AB)
Suggested Music: *The Sea* or "When You Seek Me"/*Gentle Sounds*

As Christmas approaches, there is usually increased activity in our homes. Perhaps family and friends will gather to celebrate this special time of the year. What are some of the things that you may be asked to do to prepare for this visit? When you are asked to clean your room does that mean to just shove everything under the bed and lean on the closet door to get it closed? I would imagine that you would be asked to actually do some washing or throw unneeded items away, like an old pizza box, empty soda cans, dirty sweat socks, candy wrappers.

God sent a man called John the Baptist to prepare for Jesus' coming. John begged the people to get ready for Jesus' coming by preparing their hearts to receive Jesus. John told the people to look into their hearts and to sweep away all those things that would make Jesus feel unwelcome. This is a time for us to prepare our hearts for Jesus. Let's unlock our imaginations now to visit with Jesus in the desert near Jerusalem. Perhaps we will actually be able to see John the Baptist on our journey.

1. Prepare the Way for Your Lord

Meditation

Close your eyes....Take a deep breath....Let it out slowly....
Whisper, "Jesus."....It is very quiet....You feel the warm
summer sun on your face....You are walking down a crooked
path. Rocks cut into your sandals....Sand from the desert land
sweeps over your feet as you walk....Your legs ache from the
long, tedious journey....At long last you see a group of trees
near the river....The tree limbs dance on the summer wind,
inviting you into their shade. You move more quickly now to
stand beneath the protective arms of the trees....The wind
softly pulls at your hair....Settle down onto the warm sand....
Lean against the bent olive tree....Nearby you hear the waters
of the Jordan River splashing against the shore....A large
crowd is gathered at the riverside....Near the water's edge you
see this man called John the Baptist....He is dressed in the
skins of animal animals....He urges the crowd to join him....
His firm voice is carried on the wind...."Prepare the way for
the coming of God!"....You close your eyes to rest, thinking....
"Who is this strange man? What am I to do?....How can a
person such as me prepare for the coming of God?"....John,
looking more like a beggar from the streets than God's
messenger, motions wildly with his arms....You study this
man....What does he want with you?....There is a gentle touch
on your shoulder....Jesus has joined you in the shade of the
olive tree....He smiles and calls you by name....Jesus' face
grows serious...."I would like you to meet John....My Father
has sent John to prepare the people's hearts for my coming.
Listen to John....These people have never heard of me....No
one has been baptized....You are the only person who knows
me....If God were to ask you to tell the others about me, what
would you tell them? Can you honestly say that you know me
well?"....Take a few moments to answer Jesus....(*Pause.*)

Feeling the weight of Jesus' words, you slowly make your way
down the hillside toward John....You are not sure you really
want to do this....Who is this wild man?....Jesus remains in the
shade of the tree, nodding encouragement....

"Are you the promised one?" the people ask John....John shakes his head, pointing to Jesus....John stands as you approach....He takes your hand in his....John's eyes soften.... His gaze becomes one of concern....Leaning forward, he whispers, "There is much you can do to prepare for the coming of God....Begin by looking into your own heart. Sweep away all those things that would not make Jesus feel welcome.".....

Kneeling in the warm surf, think of all those things which you have hidden from sight....all the times you may have forgotten to make someone else's road easier....You understand those things which must be swept away....Slowly make your way to where Jesus stands waiting for you....

I will leave you alone with Jesus to talk about this....Speak to Jesus remembering that he knows your heart. (*Pause until they become restless.*)

Prayer

Jesus, I have stockpiled so much garbage in my life. Help me to sort those unnecessary things out. May I be able to prepare my own heart for your coming. Do not let the shadows of my life keep me from following your path. Let your light shine through my eyes helping to light the path for others. Amen.

It is time to leave Jesus now....Turn and walk away....Take the path that runs near the cool river waters. Open your eyes and return to this room.

Discussion

You may want to suggest that each small group contemplate these questions and then be prepared to share the consensus of their answers.

- If God asked you to tell the people of your community about Jesus, what would you tell them?

- If you were the only person among your group of friends that knew Jesus, what would you want to tell them? What would you be strong enough to tell them?

- Has there been a John the Baptist in your life (someone who led you to God)?

- How will you use this Advent season to prepare for Jesus' return?

Prayer Time

Dim the lights. Background music should be played. Invite the teens to think quietly about their own lives.

Think of the rough edges that need to be sanded down. Remain in silence, keeping your eyes closed.

- Is there a rough situation at home that you want Jesus to help you with?

- Do you need to reach out to someone but you don't know how?

- Now think of those close to you who need to have Jesus' guiding hand on their shoulders.

Leader: We gather together to ask, in prayer, for your healing touch on people around the world.

Invite the teens to respond, "Lord, hear our prayer."

Leader: For all those who are suffering from an addiction of any kind, we pray to the Lord. (*Response*)

Leader: For those who are lost and can not find their way home to Jesus, we pray to the Lord. (*Response*)

Leader: For our own personal needs, we pray to the Lord. (*Allow a few minutes for them to volunteer their own prayer petitions.*) We pray that we may each find our own path to the Lord and follow it throughout our lives. For this we pray to the Lord. (*Response*)

Close by holding hands in a circle and praying the Our Father.

The Strength of Love and Faith in God

Scripture: Mt 1:18-24
Feast: Fourth Sunday of Advent (B)
**Suggested Music: *Dream Journey* or "Only a Shadow"/*Gentle
   Sounds***

Is anyone aware of the rules of marriage and engagement during the time of Joseph and Mary? To be sure, it was nothing like today's customs.

In today's society many young people seem to "put the cart before the horse." Sex is entered into lightly as recreation and not a sign of married love. Many times the obligations of both partners only go as far as pleasing themselves for the moment. Our church teaches the steps we are to take that lead to marriage and children, and yet society is teaching quite another. In today's world there is little, if any, stigma for putting the cart before the horse, but that was not the case in Palestine at the time of Jesus.

There were two parts to a Jewish marriage. First came an engagement, usually lasting a year. However, they referred to this as "being married," the groom having signed contracts with the bride's family to marry their daughter. During this time the bride and groom were not allowed to see each other. The only communication allowed was to send messages back and forth through the groom's best man. The second part, the consummation, only took place when the groom took his bride into his home following the engagement period. Joseph found Mary to be pregnant before he took her into his home and consummated the marriage. They were not living together. He knew the child could not be his. Joseph faced two choices: He could divorce her, ending the relationship, or he could go forward and accuse her of adultery. The punishment for this would have been death by public stoning.

Despite the unusual circumstances Joseph went through, he faced many of the same emotions that we might face in a similar situation. Answers to problems such as these are seldom easy. Let's release our imaginations to enable us to spend some time with Joseph and see the living proof of his faith in God.

Meditation

Close your eyes....Relax your shoulders....then your arms.... Find a comfortable position....Take a deep breath....Let it out slowly....Whisper, "Jesus."....

The day offers warm rays of sun as you enter a small village.... Stopping to rest near the village square you ask a group of men who are discussing the rise in Roman taxes, "Sirs, can you direct me to Joseph the carpenter's shop?"....Resenting the interruption the men reluctantly point the direction....The older man of the group calls out, "You a friend of Joseph?".... "Not really. But I know of him," you answer....Scratching at his unkempt beard, the man continues, "I hear Joseph's got himself quite a problem of his own."....With that the men break into loud raucous laughter....Taking the road to the right, past the village shops, you find your way to the small shop....A sign, barely visible, states, "Carpenter."....The small carpenter shop is nothing more than a loosely crafted shed made of wooden poles and bricks of hardened mud....The dirt floor of the little shop is covered with sawdust....Chisels, bits, hammers, and barrels of long nails line the walls....Joseph looks up, his long hair damp with perspiration....He uses the back of his hand to move it out of his eyes...."Good morning, friend," he says, offering you his hand in welcome....You take his hand noticing his firm but gentle grasp....He is only somewhat older than you, but lines of time and hard work crease his handsome face...."It's a warm day; care for some water from the well?" he offers, stepping out into the sun-draped yard....Joseph pulls the oaken bucket out of the well and fills a tin cup with water.... Stepping inside he hands you the cup....Joseph then continues with his work quietly now, absorbed in his own thoughts and problems....

You watch him work at his craft in silence, not knowing what your role may be this day....Finally, you interrupt, "I heard that you recently were married."...."Yes, for now. I'm sure the whole town knows this and more," he states as a matter of fact....Laying his crude saw aside, he glances up at you. "I have received disturbing news on this day, my friend," he sighs...."My wife, Mary, is pregnant and it could not be my child for I have never known her in that way....I have planned for the day she would return with me to this house but now that may all be for nothing. What shall I do?" he asks no one in particular....You walk over to Joseph's workbench, placing an arm on his shoulder, much the same way you would one of your friends....You search for an answer but are able to only stammer, "Perhaps it would be better to just end the relationship before it is too late."...."Too late for what, friend?....I love her. I can't abandon her because it is easy," he responds firmly....There is a knock on the door....The leering faces of the men from the village square intrude in the doorway. "Hear you and the wife have a little problem, eh, Joseph?" one of the gawkers asks, already knowing the answer....The second man, with long white hair, jeers out, "Sure a shame to have to stone that little beauty."....The men retreat down the road with gales of harsh laughter ringing in the air....Joseph, sitting on a three-legged stool, covers his face with his hands, "She would have been—will be—a good wife but how do I explain this to the likes of these men?"....It occurs to you that although you may have a "simple" solution, you are from a different time, a different place....Joseph stands, "Come friend, stay with me for a time. I have always tried to lead my life by God's rules, not mine—something that you should never forget."....Joseph bends low to pick up his tools and return them to their place when the walls begin to

shake with a loud pounding....Looking outside there is no one
in sight, but a large crudely lettered sign has been placed on
the front of the house, "Joseph, the fool"....You grasp the
sign and pull it down, hiding it behind your back....Joseph
wipes a tear from his eyes, pats you on the shoulder, and in a
voice barely audible says, "It's to be expected."....Joseph
wipes his brow with a rag, "I shall send a message to Mary
that I will divorce her quietly for that way she will not be
humiliated, but this does not sit well upon my heart"....
Looking in your direction he asks, "What would you do?"....
You lower your head, shaking it back and forth....Take a
moment and put yourself in Joseph's place. He is a righteous
young man but it appears that his wife has committed
adultery: a child is on its way....Think of Mary. She is
pregnant, alone, suspected of adultery, and Joseph may leave
her....Could these events happen to you or someone you care
about? (*Pause.*)

Night has fallen across the sky....The desert land becomes cold
once again as the setting sun goes to its resting place....
Joseph has invited you to stay the night and to keep him
company in his time of confusion and pain...."I will place this
problem in the hands of God," Joseph mutters as he stretches
out on the cot near the fireplace....You place a well-worn
blanket over his sorrow-riddled body....Sleep deadens the pain
of reality....Lower yourself to the floor in front of the fire,
placing your head on your arm....Sleep does not come easily
for you....In the early hours of morning Joseph becomes
restless....Although you see no one, a flimsy white haze
shrouds the small room....Joseph is speaking to a third
person, a person unseen by your eyes....There is no sound
other than Joseph's excited voice....As suddenly as it
appeared, the haze lifts from the room....Joseph sits up on the
edge of the cot rubbing his head...."Did you hear that?" he
asks....You shake your head...."I swear before all that is holy,
God sent an angel to my side."....Joseph washes his face in
the small basin of cold water sitting on a table....Joseph
smiles, his burden lightened, he flicks the towel above your
head to get your attention...."God heard my cries. He knows

my pain. On this night the angel told me to bring Mary home as my wife....The child was conceived by the Holy Spirit for she is pure and chaste."....Buckling his sandals, he continues, "Mary will give birth to a son and we shall name him Jesus. I do not understand all this but I must place trust in God."....

Joseph sees the confusion on your face...."Friend, when there is no rhyme nor reason to life's hardships, there is only one place to turn, and that is toward God....Follow God's rules, not your own rules made up to fit the situation, and he shall be faithful to you. Do not place yourself in jeopardy. Do not ask for the pain and confusion that I have carried. Do you have enough faith in God to follow his rules concerning love and marriage?" (*Pause briefly.*) Joseph places his arm loosely around your shoulders, "I knew that this was not of my doing, but could you say the same? (*Pause.*) I placed my trust in God. Would you be able to do the same?"....

I will leave you alone with Joseph for a few moments....

Prayer
My Lord, my God, my Father, hear my prayer. Like Joseph, I too at times feel alone in a world I do not understand. Keep me strong in faith. Allow me to see the path I am to follow more clearly. Remind me that you walk beside me. Amen.

As the sun rises over the desert sands the time has come for you to say goodbye....Turn and walk down the village streets....Open your eyes and return to this room.

Discussion

In either small groups or the whole group discuss the following questions:

- How do you know if God is speaking to you?

- If an angel appeared to you as it did to Joseph, would you have believed what you heard?

- If you found yourself in a situation similar to Joseph's, what path would you take?

Closing

Within the group, stack your hands together in the center of the circle. Then say, "Thank you, God, for this chance to better understand true faith and to think through my own values. Amen." Close with a group Our Father.

The Annunciation

Scripture: Mt 1:18-25; Lk 1:26-38
Feast: Fourth Sunday of Advent (AB)
Suggested Music: *Dream Journey* **or "Hail, Mary: Gentle**
Woman"/*Gentle Sounds*

Whom would you choose to deliver an extremely personal and important message for you? Friend? Teacher? Pastor? Take a few minutes and think about this. You can pick anyone currently living. Now, why would you pick this person to deliver the message?

Allow a few minutes of discussion and sharing. Then ask, "Whom would God choose to be a messenger?"

God chose the angel Gabriel to deliver one important message. Gabriel really had his work cut out for him. Not only did he deliver a message that most of us would consider earth shattering, but he also had to convince a young teenage girl that this was in everyone's best interest. Poor Gabriel! But God knew his subject well and Mary, the young girl, became our model of faith. Let's release our imaginations to be beside Mary the morning God sent Gabriel with a message that would change the world. The angel Gabriel has just awakened Mary from a sound sleep.

Meditation

Close your eyes....Take a deep breath....Feel the quiet all the way to your toes....Relax....Put aside all the sounds around you....Take one more deep breath....Whisper, "Jesus."....

3. The Annunciation

It is very early morning....The sun has just peeked over the hills of Galilee....Birds are singing their song with the light of dawn. You are curled up in your bed, covered with a tattered quilt....Mary lies still in her bed....Slowly and quietly you turn in your covers....You look over at Mary....Long dark hair surrounds her young face....Mary is your friend....You trust her....Mary suddenly sits upright, startled out of her deep sleep....You are aware of a bright light in the room....An angel stands at the foot of Mary's wooden bed!....Thoughts of alarm enter your mind, only to be dispelled by the aura of calm and peace....Mary grasps her ragged blanket about her, motioning for you to sit beside her....You feel her tremble beneath the covers....The angel speaks, "Good morning, Mary," and slowly turns to greet you....The angel calls you by name...."Do not be afraid; I have not come to harm you."....Can you hear the angel's voice?....Mary smiles at the angel....

"My name is Gabriel," the angel says gently....Gabriel turns now to speak to Mary....Listen as he speaks...."Do not be afraid, Mary; God has sent me to tell you that a male child is about to be born....When the child is born he is to be named Jesus, a name that means 'Yahweh saves'"....Mary glances toward you, her eyes large and round, her mouth open....The angel gently puts his hand upon Mary's shoulder. "God asks if you are willing to be this child's mother," Gabriel adds....With no hesitation, Mary nods her head, "Yes"....Then looking at Gabriel, she asks, "How can this be? Joseph has not yet taken me into his home."....The bright light surrounding the angel glows in her eyes....Gabriel reaches down and touches Mary's dark curls...."God wants you to be this child's mother, and he will perform a miracle....Your child will be called the Son of God....But if you are not willing to do this..."....The angel's words are frozen in mid-air....Mary scoots to the edge of her bed, falling to her knees in prayer....The lovely young woman reaches out her hand for you to kneel beside her....You feel the cold, hard floor beneath your legs but Mary's hands are warm, her face glowing....Mary speaks, "Whatever God asks of me, I will do....I do not understand but I will trust in God....I will be the mother of this child."....

The angel smiles warmly at Mary and disappears as quickly as he appeared....Mary takes your hand in hers once more....She rises to sit up on the bed....Mary wraps your cold legs in the well-worn blanket....Look up into her eyes, ready to speak.... Mary knows what you are about to ask and answers...."We must put our whole trust in God at times."....

Take this time to speak to Mary....Ask her anything you want....Remember that she always hears your prayers....Mary will help you to trust in God's wisdom for your life....The mother of God will hear your prayer.... (*Pause until they grow restless.*)

Prayer
Dearest Mary, I fall to my knees before you. I honor you as the mother of God. I love you for your faith, trust, and strength. Guide me on my walk with the Lord. Let me not stumble and lose my way. Amen.

It is time to leave Mary's side....Mary wraps her arms about you, holding you close....Say goodbye....Turn and leave the room, walking out into the early morning mist....Open your eyes and return to this room.

Discussion

I would like to ask the girls this question. I will give you a few minutes to think about your answers.

- Put yourself in Mary's place. You are very young, unmarried, pregnant, accused of adultery, and the man you love is thinking of leaving you. How would you feel? How would your faith in God enter into this situation?

- Young men, I ask this question of you. If you were in Joseph's shoes, what would your reaction be to all of the above? How would your faith in God play a part in your decisions?

- From the position of both Joseph and Mary, what would you say to God, knowing the consequences of your answer?

Ask the girls to share first, then the boys. Everyone should answer the third question.

Prayer Time

Light a large candle. Place a rose, silk or fresh, beside the candle. Play background music. Provide pencils and paper. If appropriate, insert the pink candle in the Advent wreath and light it. Ask someone to read Mark 13:33-37.

The story of Mary and Joseph is one of absolute trust in God. Mary was not much more than a child herself, yet she had the wisdom and faith to say "Yes" to God. God is waiting for us to say "Yes" to what he asks of us in our lives. Pause for a moment to think about the area of your life in which you need to reach out with faith and say "Yes" to God.

Ask the teens to write their responses, then invite the teens to come forward to place the folded paper into a sealed gift box.

Optional: You may want to include the gift box during the presentation of the gifts at the upcoming Sunday Mass.

Leader: Mary, by your example we begin to understand the meaning of faith. We come before you with our dreams, hopes, problems, and prayers. "Blessed is the fruit of thy womb, Jesus."

God loved us so much that he sent his only Son to us.

We open our hearts and lives to the love of God. We are called to be a community bonded together by God's love for us and our love for others.

Invite the young people to offer individual prayers of petition and ask them to respond, "Lord of wonder, Lord of light, hear our prayer."

The Birth of Jesus

Scripture: Lk 2:1-16
Feast: Christmas (ABC)
Suggested Music: "When You See Me"/*Gentle Sounds* or "Some Children See Him"/*December*

It came to pass in the days of Caesar Augustus, the ruler of Rome, that a law was passed requiring everyone within his reign to be counted. The farmers, carpenters, weavers, elders all traveled to the town where they were born, to record their names and the names of all the people in their families in a book of census. While Joseph and Mary were in Joseph's hometown, Bethlehem, the time came for Mary to give birth to her first-born son. Let us release our imaginations to walk with Mary and Joseph in the joy of this season.

Meditation

Find a comfortable position....Become very still....Close out the sounds of those around you....Let your body relax....Travel to the days of long ago....Take a deep breath....Whisper, "Jesus."....Feel the quiet cover you like a warm blanket....

It is just before sunset....The day is about to be clouded with the hand of darkness....You have walked many miles today.... Your legs grow weary, your burdens heavy....You can see the flickering lights of Bethlehem ahead....Clip-clop, clip-clop, the donkey's hooves beat a rhythm on the dusty trail....The air is cold and filled with the smoke of weary travelers' campfires....

Joseph the carpenter, looking not much older than you, walks beside you, his dark hair falling to his shoulders...."The city is going to be very crowded. I hope there is a room for us," he

24

says to his pregnant wife....Mary, seated on the back of an old grey donkey, smiles and pulls her cloak around her....Mary looks very tired, her body rocking back and forth with the rhythm of the donkey....As you draw close to the city, Joseph hands you the reins of his donkey....He asks you to look after Mary....Joseph hurries ahead to find a place to stay for the evening....Lead the donkey carrying Mary through the gates of the city....There are more people than you have ever seen before....People are pushing and shoving, the strain of travel showing on their faces....You almost lose your grip on the donkey's reins as you are shoved to the ground....Mary shudders and lets out a sigh....

At last Joseph returns....Worry and sadness are spoken through Joseph's heavy steps....Joseph is unable to find a place to stay....Mary leans down and speaks softly in Joseph's ear....You realize that it is time for the child to be born.... "Look after Mary," Joseph says to you as he hurries through the crowds...."God be with you," you call after Joseph....Mary lets out a deep sigh and reaches out to touch your shoulder.... "The child is coming soon!" Mary tells you....Silently, you ask for God's protection and guidance....There must be shelter somewhere....

Joseph is turned away from every house and every inn....You leave Mary's side, determined to help....Knocking on the back door of an inn, you beg the innkeeper to help find shelter for Mary....The innkeeper reluctantly motions down the road where there is a cave....He tells you that frequently animals are kept inside out of the weather there, but it is clean and dry....Run to share the news with Mary and Joseph....The three of you set out toward the cave, down the crowded roadway, through the throngs of people, past the olive grove, until at last you see the cave....

Joseph gently lifts the small figure of Mary down from the bony back of the donkey. Joseph speaks firmly, "Friend, go ahead and make a bed for Mary in the fresh hay."....Quickly gather the dry hay into a pile....Then smooth it out with your hands....The sweet smell of hay fills your nostrils....A small lamb nestles against his mother for warmth....From within the darkness of the cave, a cow's mournful voice sounds....God's creatures have also found shelter here from the cold night air....Joseph guides Mary to the makeshift bed you have prepared for her....

Leave Mary and Joseph alone now....For this is their time.... This is God's time....In a corner of the cave you lay back on the hay....The sheep move toward your warmth in the darkness of night....You begin to pray....The presence of God surrounds you....God is here!....In the still of the long night you hear a baby's soft cry....A cry that will someday bring the world to its knees....Joseph stands beside you...."The child is a boy. His name shall be Jesus," he tells you....Joseph leads you to Mary's resting place....

Mary smiles as you enter....The baby is resting in her arms.... Joseph strokes the child's head....You look at Jesus....He is small; he is perfect....A tear of wonder, a tear of joy falls gently upon your cheek....Kneel before him....Give thanks to God....Mary rises on one elbow and invites you to come closer....She holds out her newborn son for you to hold.... "Would you like to hold Jesus?" she asks....Settle close to Mary as she places the sleeping child in your arms....You are nervous....You are filled with wonder....Take a moment to feel the warmth of the child in your arms, to feel the miracle of birth....Mary leans close, "What can we do for you, my dear friend?"....Share this holy night with Jesus, Mary, and Joseph.... (*Pause until the teens grow restless.*)

Prayer

Jesus, in the stillness of this night I have held you with my arms. God's Son has blessed me with his presence. The tiny hands of Jesus held my fingers and my heart. Welcome to our world. Amen.

If you listen very closely, you can hear the angels in heaven singing songs of praise to God...."Glory to God in the highest and peace on earth to people of good will."

It is now early morning....Crowds have gathered outside the cave....Shepherds from the nearby fields are offering praise to God. The shepherds tell of an angel who appeared to them, bringing news of great joy, "In the city of Bethlehem, a savior has been born for you. This savior is Christ the Lord."

It is time for you to leave this night of wonder....Bend low and kiss the cheek of baby Jesus. In time to come you will wipe away his tears and his blood from this cheek. Press the child's dimpled hand against your mouth....Rise, turn and walk away through the entrance of the cave, out into the misty dawn.... Open your eyes and return to this room.

Prayer Service

You may photocopy the prayer service on the next two pages to distribute to each person.

Dim the lights. Light one large candle. Hand out the prayer service. Divide the young people into two groups, asking each group to slowly read its part together. After the groups have read their parts, you may wish to conclude with the following discussion questions.

Discussion (Optional)

- How can we give the gift of Jesus to others?

- What is your favorite part of the Christmas story? Why?

Prayer Service: The Birth of Jesus

Leader: In the stillness of this night, we gather to welcome the child Jesus into our world.

Group One:

> O, little town of Bethlehem,
> how still we see thee lie;
> above thy deep and dreamless sleep
> the silent stars go by;
> yet in thy dark street shineth
> the everlasting light.
> The hopes and fears of all the years
> are met in thee tonight.

Leader: Joseph and Mary, models of faith, became the parents of our living God. We fall to our knees before the manger of Christ our Lord.

Group Two:

> Away in a manger,
> no crib for a bed,
> the little Lord, Jesus,
> lay down his sweet head.

Leader: The angels have sung on high. God has sent his only Son as our gift on this night.

Group One:

> It came upon the midnight clear,
> that glorious song of old,
> from angels bending near the earth,
> to touch their harps of gold;
> "Peace on the earth, good will to men
> from heaven's all gracious King."

Leader: From the barren hills the shepherds came bearing only the gift of wonder and love.

This prayer service is taken from *Guided Meditations for Teens* by Sydney Ann Merritt © 1997 Resource Publications, Inc. All rights reserved.

Group Two:

>Silent night, holy night!
>All is calm, all is bright
>round yon virgin mother and child!
>Holy infant so tender and mild,
>sleep in heavenly peace.

Leader: Let us pray together.
Blessed are we because of your birth
We sing your praise to people of all nations.

Response: Joy to the world! The Lord is come!

Leader: On this night we are filled with joy and hope
for unto us, a Savior was born.

Response: Joy to the world! The Lord is come!

Leader: Help us to live our lives reflecting the light
of your grace, the charity of your heart, and the
love of your Father in heaven. Amen.

Response: Joy to the world! The Lord is come!

The Feast of Epiphany

Scripture: Mt 2:1-12
Feast: Epiphany (ABC)
Suggested Music: *Dream Journey* or "Some Children See
Him"/*December* or "Canyon of the Moon"/*Another Star in*
the Sky

During the time of Jesus, people believed a new star appeared
in the sky each time a child was born. One night a group of
wise men, educated and knowledgeable people, spotted an
extremely bright star in the sky, which, according to them,
meant that someone very important had been born on that
night. Little did they know how correct they were.
Remembering the ancient Scriptures, they believed that surely
the Messiah had been born. They set out on their search,
following the star. According to Scripture, these men were not
Jewish but were from the east. Perhaps Matthew was trying to
tell us that Jesus was born for everyone, not just the Jews.

Let's release our imaginations, joining the wise men in their
search for the baby born in a simple stable, our Lord of Lords,
Jesus.

Meditation

Find a comfortable position....Shrug your shoulders, releasing
the day's tensions....Let stillness settle within you....Take a
deep breath....Let it out slowly....Put everything else out of
your mind....

With eyes from within your mind, look into the ancient past, a
time following the birth of Christ....You are near the gates of
the city of Jerusalem....It is evening....Glowing lanterns light

up the shops and houses....People are scurrying about, gathering their belongings....Watch the activity for a few seconds....Donkeys loaded with the city's treasure push past you, through the gate....A small group of men approaches the city....They glance upward several times, pointing to the sky....A tall, dark-skinned man dressed in a flowing red cloak speaks to you, "Where is the newborn King of the Jews?".... His voice is harsh, clouded with mystery....Before you can answer, he stops a band of merchants...."Where is the King of the Jews?....We have seen his star in the east and have come to worship him."....You have heard rumors about the baby born in a stable....Go up to the travelers, offering to go with them on their journey...."Welcome, friend. But first we must eat. Will you watch our belongings?"....The men, bearing dust and fatigue from their journey, leave their colts and three wrapped packages with you....You settle down on your haunches, waiting....

A small group of King Herod's soldiers, their swords shining in the moonlight, question citizens, asking, "Where is the Messiah? Where was he born?"....One soldier, his lantern swinging from side to side, runs off toward King Herod's castle....You shudder in the cold evening air....

The three wise men join you now, packing their belongings onto the backs of the mules....Suddenly, you hear a trumpet's sounding voice...."The King is coming! The King is coming!" shout the soldiers....King Herod steps from his horse....Save one, you have never seen a king this close....He is dressed in bright blue velvet....A crown of gold sits upon his head of black curls....He is a large man with a booming voice....The ground seems to shake when he speaks....By now, many people have gathered around the king, including leaders of the Jewish people...."Where is this Messiah to be born?" the king growls....The wise men answer, "The sacred Scriptures tell us that the Messiah will be born in Bethlehem."

The king walks back and forth, strutting his power....Beneath the cape of royalty lies a person of insecurity, one determined to maintain his kingdom at any cost....Turning to the wise

31

men he roars, "Tell me the exact time you first noticed the star."....The king now turns toward you, "Go and find out all you can about the child. When you have found him, come back and tell me so I may go also and worship him."....The men from the east gather about the king, encouraging him on his quest....But from within your being, you shudder, knowing full well the king plots death for this newborn child....

You step back out of view, once again joining the three men from the east....As night settles its cloak of darkness across the land, you and the wise men begin your journey over the desert sands....The night sky is darkened except for the brilliant light of the star....The star appears to travel just ahead of the journeyers....its brilliance casting a stream of light across the night sky...."This must be the sign everyone is talking about," you think to yourself....Everyone talks at once, pointing excitedly to the sky...."What will you bring the new king?" one voice calls out in the night air...."I have brought a gift of rare perfume, one only the rich can afford."....Your hands quickly scan your pockets....Surely, you will find the baby king and have nothing to offer him....

After many hours of travel in the stillness of the night, you reach Bethlehem....The star now shines more brilliantly than before....It lights your way through the cobblestone streets and rows of little houses....The only sounds you hear are the clip-clops of the donkey's hooves and the quiet, almost reverent, shuffling of footsteps....Specks of light seep from the cracks around the doorway. At last the star appears to have stopped moving across the sky....The path of light now falls upon a small cave, almost hidden in the shadows....The glow of a lantern flickers from within....A crude wooden door covers the entrance to the stable....Sheep and cows lie upon the cold earth near the entrance...The wise men whisper in the darkness...."This is where we will find the Messiah".... Looking toward you, they order, "Go now and knock on the door....Tell the child's parents we have come to worship their newborn son, the promised Messiah."....You make your way to the doorway of the cave....Put your ear to the door....Soft

sounds of an infant's cooing travel on the cold night air....
Knock on the makeshift door....Knock again....The man called
Joseph stands in the doorway....He greets you warmly,
offering his callused hands....Tell Joseph why you have
come....Joseph peeks out the door, then waves, inviting the
three wise men to come inside....

Joseph shows you into a dimly lit corner of the stable....Mary
sits upon a bed made of straw, wrapped in the warmth of a
woven blanket....Nearby, the child Jesus lies in a makeshift
cradle....Mary takes your hand, leading you to the babe....
Look closely at the tiny child as his hand wraps around your
little finger....He is so small, so perfect....Your heart
pounds....This is the Lord....This is your Savior....Fall upon
your knees, giving thanks to God for showing you the path to
Jesus....The warm rush of love flows through your body....

The wise men kneel at the foot of the manger, giving their
thanks to God....The gold shines in the light of a nearby
lantern....The gifts of frankincense and myrrh lie yet
unopened....Mary smiles at you, "His name is Jesus," she says
warmly....You dig into your pockets once again....Surely there
must be something that you can offer as a gift to the infant
lying in his mother's arms....

I will leave you for a moment with Mary, Joseph, and the
infant Jesus....Look into the child's eyes....These are not the
eyes of an ordinary child; the past and the future of life itself
come from within his gaze....Speak to Jesus with your
heart....He will know the gift that you are to offer him....You
may be able to offer nothing of monetary value, but something
more precious than a gift wrapped in gold....Perhaps it will be
the talents you were given, the kindness and gentleness of
love, or a promise that will lie within your heart....

Prayer

*Dear sweet Jesus, I, like King Herod, have things in
my life that I am reluctant to give up. I do not know
why these things have importance to me. There are
times when I have followed the wrong star to a place*

*hidden in darkness. Light my path. Carry my burdens.
Accept my love. Amen.*

The sun is rising above the rooftops, replacing the cold dark of
night with the warmth and light of a new day....The wise men
have begun their journey back to their homeland....It is time
for you to leave now....Say goodbye to Mary, Joseph, and the
infant Jesus....

Walk out the splintered wooden door of the stable....A rooster
crows in the distance, welcoming another day....Open your
eyes and return to this room....

Discussion

In groups of four, discuss the answers to the following
questions:

- What star are you following in your own life?

- Like the magi, would you be able to drop everything else
  and just follow the path to Jesus?

- The three wise men gave the best gifts they could possibly
  give to the child Jesus. If Jesus were born today, what gift
  would you offer him?

Closing

*Dim the room, lighting one large candle. (Optional: Place
votive candles for each student in five-ounce paper cups.
Ask students to come forward to light their candles off the
large candle.)*

Leader: On this day, we come together to remember the wise
       men of long ago who chose to follow your star. The
       wise men offered gifts of gold, incense and myrrh.
       We, too, must look to the heavens and follow the
       path of his star.

5. The Feast of Epiphany

Please come forward to light your candle from the flame of this community candle. The light that our candles give is a visible sign of the light of your presence among us.

Invite the teens to respond, "You are with us, Lord."

Leader: May we find your light shining within us. (*Response*)

Leader: Direct our path, light our way through life. (*Response*)

Leader: We offer you our gift of love,
    our prayers of hope,
    and faith held dearly within our hearts. (*Response*)

All: Christ be with us, Lord be with us.

Greet each other with a sign of peace.

The Baptism of Our Lord

Scripture: Mt 3:11-17; Mk 1:7-11; Lk 3:15-16,21-22
Feast: Baptism of the Lord (ABC)
Suggested Music: *The Sea* or "By Name I Have Called
     You"/*Gentle Sounds*

Who was John the Baptist? What was John's purpose in
regard to Jesus? Would you agree that God provides a John
the Baptist, perhaps several if we are stubborn, in our own
lives? Who has been John the Baptist in your life, preparing
you to meet the Lord?

Jesus, the Son of God and sinless, chose to be baptized by
John along with hundreds of others. Why would Jesus take
this step? Jesus, hearing that John the Baptist was preaching
near the Jordan River, decided to go and listen to John talk.
At the end of the talk, Jesus walked into the waters of the
Jordan River to be baptized along with all the people standing
within earshot of John's preaching. John asked that each one
give up their sinful lives and follow the coming Messiah's path.
Let's release our imaginations now as you join Jesus near the
shores of the Jordan River.

Meditation

Close your eyes....Find a comfortable position....Allow your
body to feel limp and relaxed....Shut out the sounds of the
day....Imagine the sounds of water flowing down a mountain
creek, and the life it gives....It is calm, it is peaceful here....
You are sitting on a hillside covered with a carpet of new

grass....The sweet smell of a recent rain fills your nostrils....
The sun warms the back of your neck and shoulders....This
will be a good day!....

Look out far below....The blue-green waters of the Jordan
River wash against the sandy shore....The valley is brown and
barren except for a few small trees....You do not want to leave
this spot high above the valley floor....But it is time to make
your way down the hillside....

Walk carefully down the path....Your feet slip and slide out of
control on the loose rocks beneath your feet....You hear
footsteps not far behind you...."May I walk with you?" a gentle
voice calls out....Turning, you see it is Jesus....Jesus calls your
name, smiling warmly...."Come, let me steady you so you
don't slip on the path."....Place your hand on Jesus' strong
arm....His skin is bronzed from days in the desert sun....It is
good to see your friend again....

You are nearly at the bottom of the hillside when Jesus points
to a large crowd gathered on the shore...."All of those people
have come to be baptized by my cousin, John."....Jesus steps
up his pace....You are almost running to keep up with him....
Clouds of sand cover your feet as your stride lengthens....
"There is John. He is standing in the river near the shore,"
Jesus says excitedly....John is wearing an animal skin....A
rope belt is pulled tightly about his waist....His hair is long and
uncombed....People are wading out into the river waters....
John is bent over now, his hands cupped, dipping into the
water....A young woman, about your age, stands in front of
John....John pours the refreshing water over her head....She
is smiling and happy, her long hair falling into wet ringlets....
Questions cloud your mind....Jesus, knowing your questions,
answers, "These people are asking John to baptize them so
that they may put aside those situations which should not be
in their lives. John baptizes them to strengthen them with
God's Spirit so that they might be ready for my coming."....
Questions continue to fill your mind....

"Walk with me, friend. John shall baptize me, also." Jesus motions for you to follow...."We will ask John to baptize you, with your permission, and then myself."....Still grasping Jesus' arm, you step into the cool waters of the Jordan River.... Jagged rocks cut into your bare feet....Long fingers of seaweed wrap about your legs....The river waters, chilled by the long autumn nights, pound against the shore, knocking you off balance....Jesus reaches forward, steadying your step....The water is so cold it leaves a burning feeling, and then numbness....John the Baptist glances up into your eyes, smiles, and calls out your name....He places his large, rough hands on your shoulder...."I am baptizing you with this water, but someone is coming who is greater than I....I am not worthy of tying his sandals....He will baptize you with the Holy Spirit."....John once again dips his hands into the frigid water, then slowly pours it over your head....Shocking first, the life-giving waters spill down your face....Lick your lips....Taste the water....A surge of warmth flows through your body....Dip your hand in the water....Splash your face once again....Jesus smiles, then takes his place before John....

Jesus, standing, bows his head....A tear forms on John's cheek, perhaps a tear of recognition, a tear of joy....John looks startled, "Jesus, you should baptize me."....Jesus shakes his head "No," then speaks in a whisper to John....Jesus raises his hands in prayer as John begins to pour the water over Jesus' head....

As Jesus stands raising his hands to the heavens, his cloak heavy with water, the clouds begin to separate....A beautiful dove appears above Jesus' head....Listen to the silence....In the quiet of the moment you hear the gentle brush of angels' wings signaling the voice of God....A voice from beyond the clouds announces, "This is my Son. I love him."....Sounds of awe fill the air; people fall to their knees in reverence to God....

Jesus turns and, placing an arm on your shoulder, leads you to shore....Walk a short distance around the water's edge....Jesus stops near a pile of driftwood....He speaks quietly, "God has called you by name....The Holy Spirit of God rests within your heart."....The pounding of your heart echoes in your ears.... "You will have the strength and joy to share your knowledge of me with others."....Jesus settles against a boulder, warming himself in the last rays of the sun...."Remember that God has chosen you and called you by name to carry the message of the kingdom of God."....You struggle against the burden of his words, "I am nothing special. I am too young to be of service to God....My friends will turn away from me, laughing....What can I offer him?" you ask....The Lord smiles....Taking your hand in his and leaning close, he whispers, "I will show you the way; new strengths will begin to emerge....Will you share your life with me?"

Take this time to be with Jesus.... (*Pause until the young people grow restless.*)

Prayer

Jesus, show me the way to God's kingdom. I am weak and frail against the strife of life. Strengthen me with your Holy Spirit to enable me to reflect your light to others. Amen.

It is time to leave....Lay your hand upon his....Even the touch leaves his warmth flowing through you....Tell Jesus goodbye for now....Walk down the rock-strewn beach.... Open your eyes and return to this room....

Discussion

- As you stood with Jesus in the waters of the Jordan River, what did your baptism mean to you?

- How important do you consider the events of Jesus' baptism? Of your own baptism?

Prayer Service

You may prefer to use this prayer service rather than discussion time.

Gather the teens in a circle. Dim the lights, lighting one large candle in the center of the room. On the table place two large bowls of water, a white garment, and a baptismal candle. Explain that candles remind us that God calls us to live in the light of Jesus.

Leader: We are brothers and sisters in God's family. Let us renew the promise of our baptism to live as Jesus did, always attempting to follow the path of the Lord. Do you believe God, our creator, wants us to be happy?

Invite the teens to respond, "I do! Alleluia!"

Leader: Do you believe in Jesus? (*Response*)

Leader: Do you believe in the Holy Spirit, who lives within us to enrich our own potential? (*Response*)

Leader: Do you believe that after we die we shall rise again with Jesus to live with God forever? (*Response*)

Leader: God is calling each of us by name. Help us to follow his path in faith. Amen.

Invite the young people to come forward and dip both their hands in the water, first with fists clenched, demonstrating how hard it is to always live as Christians, then slowly opening their hands, inviting the Spirit of God to work through them. Then they should sign themselves and say, "I am a child of God. God loves me."

Part II

Lent, Triduum, & Easter

Hurricane of Evil

Scripture: Mt 4:1-11; Mk 1:12-15; Lk 4:1-13
Feast: First Sunday of Lent (A)
**Suggested Music: *Dream Journey* or "When You Seek
    Me"/*Gentle Sounds***

*Form small groups of four. Ask the groups to form a list of
temptations that would be the hardest for them to resist.
Ask each group to participate by sharing their list and
consensus of answers to the following questions:*

- What kinds of things would you find most tempting?

- When do you find yourself most vulnerable to be tempted?
  What makes you stress to the max?

Did Jesus ever find himself tempted? Of course, he did. Satan
tried to seduce Jesus when he seemed to be at his weakest.
Satan took a look at Jesus and thought, "This guy is tired,
hungry, and pretty miserable. Now is the time to pull out all
the stops."

As Jesus was baptized, the sky opened and the Spirit of God
descended like a dove. Jesus was then led by the Spirit into
the desert to be tempted by the devil. In keeping with the
Jewish custom of fasting, Jesus did not eat from sunrise to
sundown for forty days. Jesus was seeking guidance from the
Father. Within your small group, make yourself comfortable,
release your imagination, close your eyes, and journey into the
desert with Jesus.

Meditation

The desert sands sweep across the arid land, forming tall
funnels of granular earth rising into the sky....Jesus walks
ahead of you....He is unaware of your presence....Hunger
grips your stomach....The sun's rays create a haze over the
endless sand....Heat waves rise on the crest of the distant
hills....Jesus suddenly stops short, falling onto the hot sand....
Carrying a small flask of water, you run to his side....As
though not seeing you, he sits motionless....His lips are
cracked and bleeding from the sun....Wet a small handkerchief
with drops of the precious life-giving water....Press it against
Jesus' lips....For an instant he holds your hand to his lips....

The sky darkens....Ill winds blow....An image stands before
you—not man, not beast....His lips curve in a knowing
smile....Jesus rises, pushing himself between you and this
vision of temptation....You are an observer, nothing else....
You are powerless to move or make a decision....A taunting
voice of evil speaks, "If you truly are the Son of God, tell these
stones to become bread."....Jesus, wiping the sand from his
parched lips replies, "Man does not live on bread alone, but
on every word that comes from the mouth of God."....Satan,
angered by this, wraps an arm around Jesus, whisking him
away from harsh reality....

Satan takes Jesus to the highest point in the holy city, the
Temple....You follow them, caught in Satan's evil hurricane....
"If you are the Son of God, then throw yourself down," Satan
demands of Jesus. "For it is written: 'He will command his
angels concerning you, and they will lift you up in their hands,
so that you will not strike your foot against a stone.'"....Jesus,
growing tired, answers, "It is also written: 'Do not put the
Lord your God to the test.'"....Angered, Satan takes Jesus to
the top of the highest mountain....Jesus stands near the
crumbling edge, boulders eaten by time...."Look below. See all
the kingdoms of the world and all of their splendor. All this I
will give you," the devil says with a broad sweep of his arm....
"This is yours if you will bow down and worship me."....

Jesus looks far into the valley below, shakes his head, then turns to his tempter, "Away from me, Satan! For it is written, 'Worship the Lord your God, and serve him only.'"....Jesus falls to his knees in prayer....Clouds form a protective blanket around him....Jesus, noticing you crouched in the mountain grasses, smiles and walks toward you. "It is time to leave this place." Placing his arm around your shoulders, he leads you down the mountain side, coming to rest near a small creek.... Dip your hand into the cool waters....Jesus presses his lips into the bubbling water...."My friend, I too, am not without temptation....What I have faced today is no different than those things that tempt you....Think for a moment of all the things that the world offers, those things that will mean nothing tomorrow: Doing harm to your own body with drugs or alcohol....parties that bring no lasting joy....a fast car....the philosophy of life, 'If it feels good, do it,'....stolen sex in a back seat....I, too, felt the cold sweat of fear, all the anxieties, and even all the temptations that you have experienced. I turned to my Father for protection and guidance. Speak to me, my child....How may I help you to get past this point?....What is your greatest temptation right now? How can I help you?"

I will leave you alone with Jesus to talk about this. Think about all those times you find it hard to resist following in the footsteps of others....Let Jesus help.

Prayer

Remind me to always seek your guidance. Help me to resist those things that will take me into harm's way. Thank you for your forgiveness and patience. Amen.

Discussion

- What have you found most helpful in resisting temptation?
- If this group could help you during the coming week to resist falling victim to temptation, what would that be?

Prayer Service: "I give these things to you"

Supplies: paper, pencils, petri dish, background music
Optional: small amount of kitty litter for bottom of dish

Pass out slips of paper and pencils. Ask them to write down, in silence, the areas of their lives that are most affected by temptation or an area that they believe needs strengthening. Instruct that the folded papers will be dropped into the petri dish, one person at a time, and in the order they feel comfortable with.

Remain in silence. Kneel, hold hands, and pray the Our Father.

Play "When You Seek Me"/Gentle Sounds or Dream Journey.

The Cloak of God

Scripture: Mk 9:2-10; Lk 9:28-36a
Feast: Second Sunday of Lent (ABC)
Suggested Music: *Dream Journey* or "Eye That Has Not
    Seen"/*Instruments of Peace*

Does anyone remember seeing a preview of a coming movie, perhaps one that really appealed to you? How about a Sunday night sports program that previews game highlights and offers comments on next week's games? These previews whet your appetite, don't they? Do you suppose Jesus ever resorted to a trick like that—something to get people's interest aroused? Many Jewish people, including the apostles, were expecting a political Messiah. Because Jesus wasn't a political leader, he used the "preview" events to tell the apostles that he was indeed the Messiah. With Jesus' death in the near future, the apostles needed reassurance that Jesus was the Messiah and that the kingdom of God on earth was at hand. But seeing is not always believing.

One day Jesus gave a few of his friends a preview of what the kingdom of God would be like after the resurrection.

Jesus and his disciples spent six days speaking to people in villages around Philippi. They were very tired of travel and the crowds. The disciples were surprised when Jesus invited his friends, Peter, James, and John, to join him in climbing to a high mountaintop. Let's free our imaginations, joining Jesus and his friends in what turned out to be an amazing journey.

Meditation

Find a comfortable position....Close your eyes....Feel your
hands go limp....Take a deep breath in....Now let your breath
out slowly....Whisper, "Jesus."....Relax.

You are climbing a very steep hill....The muscles in your legs
burn with each push forward. Your foot slips on a rolling
stone....The sun's rays beat down your back....Beads of
perspiration fall from your brow....Jesus walks ahead of you....
He turns and motions for you to hurry and join him....James
sits down upon a weathered tree stump, trying to catch his
breath....Peter, the oldest, pushes past you to speak with
Jesus....Listen to Peter's puffing and panting....You smile to
yourself....Jesus calls back to you, "Did you ever see a more
beautiful day?"...."Can we stop for a while?" you ask. Jesus
turns smiling, "We will soon be at the top. Don't waste time
complaining. Enjoy the beauty that God has given to you."....
Pausing momentarily, Jesus points to the valley below and the
sky above, "It could all be taken away in a moment's notice."
(*Pause briefly.*)

At long last, you arrive at the mountain's crest....It is almost
flat....Huge boulders of rocks burst free of the mountain's
grasp, casting long shadows in the moonlight. The wind is
blowing your hair, blushing your cheeks with its cool breath....
Jesus drops to his knees and begins to pray....Looking over
his shoulder, Jesus speaks to you and the disciples, "Join me
now in prayer, giving thanks to God for our many
blessings."....Peter murmurs, "It's about time we rest," as he
drops to the ground, folding his legs beneath him. Peter
lowers his head, touching the ground with his forehead in
prayer, according to the custom of the day....Soon all fall
asleep except you and Jesus....

Use this time to think of all the wonderful gifts that God has
given you....a family....a home....friends....Think of the
goodness God has provided you....Give thanks to God for
these gifts. (*Pause briefly.*) Peter's grumbling has stopped and

you see a smile on his weather-beaten face as he falls into deep slumber....Put your head down now in prayer....

Feel the presence of a warm glow....Look up....It is the brightest light that you have ever seen....Cup your hands over your eyes....Jesus remains kneeling, glowing in the light....His clothes become as white as new-fallen snow....Rub your eyes....Jesus is talking to two old men...."How did they get up to the mountaintop?" you ask yourself. Peter has come to his feet, his mouth wide open at the wonder of what he sees before him....He cries out, "It is Moses and Elijah; they have returned from the dead!"

Jesus is speaking to Elijah, the prophet of Jesus' coming, and God's favored leader, Moses....Strain to hear what they are saying....The three men of God are discussing how Jesus is going to die in Jerusalem....Can you hear them?....You shudder, knowing these words are not for your ears....Your heart is pounding with fear....What is happening?....Peter's mouth moves a mile a minute, talking on and on about putting up buildings....James covers his eyes, shielding them from the light....James whispers in your ear, "Peter is frightened too; he just doesn't always know what else to do or say so he keeps on talking."....

In an instant the shadow of a cloud appears and covers everyone with its soft, billowing arms....You cannot see above or below....There is just the cloud....Even Peter is quiet now....A deep voice comes from the cloud, "This is my Son, whom I love. Listen to him"....Surely this must be the voice of God! The cloud lifts from the mountaintop....Only Jesus remains....You and James, John, and Peter huddle together, talking of what you have seen this day....

It is now nearly dark as the four of you and Jesus make your way down the mountainside. Loose rocks cause you to stumble....Darkness is closing in....Jesus stops and turns to you, offering his hand....Look up into Jesus' eyes, questioning what you have seen....He winks and places his finger across his lips...."Shhh!"....

Jesus stops by a clump of trees to rest....Inviting you to join him, he says, "You have walked with me this day. You have experienced the wonder of the transfiguration and now I ask you this simple question....Do you believe?....Will you serve me? Will you place your life in my hands and in my heart?"....I will leave you alone with Jesus. Look into your heart and speak to Jesus. (*Pause for a minute or until they grow restless.*)

Prayer

Dearest Jesus: I, like your apostles, still have difficulty believing and understanding what you want of me.
Bless me with wisdom to know what you ask of me.
Fill me with faith, faith enough to reach beyond myself to serve you. Amen.

You are at the bottom of the mountain now....It is time for you to leave....Turn and wave goodbye....Remember this time with Jesus....Open your eyes and return to this room.

Discussion

- Has there ever been a time in your life when Jesus appeared to you in a special way?

- Why do you think that Jesus took only three of the apostles with him? Why these three?

- How could this experience help the apostles to understand Jesus' being the Messiah?

Closing

Stand. Lights low, light a candle. Play background music.

Divide teens into two groups. Invite students to pray the Apostle's Creed in echo format.

Optional: Pray the Our Father together, stacking hands in the center of the group.

Justice Begins in Your Own Heart

Scripture: Jn 2:13-25
Feast: Third Sunday of Lent (B)
Suggested Music: *Dream Journey* or "I Will Never Forget You"/*Gentle Sounds*

Has there been a recent news story or event in your neighborhood that demonstrated a lack of justice? What happened? Did it make you want to do something about it or did it make you feel helpless to change the situation? What did you want to do about it? Can anger be constructive? What would it take to push you into action? Don't talk the talk if you can't walk the walk.

Do you suppose that Jesus ever felt that kind of anger? What would trigger his anger? Is it ever enough to just feel incensed? In order to walk his walk we may need to see how Jesus handled injustice.

The only place where Jews could offer sacrifices to God was in the Temple and they believed they should offer only the most fit of animals as a sacrifice because God deserves only the best. At times the priests and cagey merchants used this belief to cheat the poor. Unscrupulous people have roamed the earth since time began.

The victims of their scams were usually the poor who were unable to protect themselves. For example, one common scam involved the poor Jewish shepherd who would pick out his best sheep to take to the Temple to serve as an offering to God. When he arrived at the Temple, the priest would inspect the animal and state that it was unfit. The shepherd then had the choice of making the long trip home for another animal or to follow the priest's suggestion of purchasing a "guaranteed perfect" animal from the merchant just beyond the Temple gates. However, the cost was very high. The priest who rejected the first animal would receive a cut from the merchant for sending the shepherd to his stall.

Moneychangers also set up tables in the area. The pilgrims had to pay a Temple tax with Jewish currency. They could not use Roman coins because they were engraved with the image of the emperor, whom the Romans worshiped as a god. The moneychangers made huge profits by exchanging the Roman coins for less than they were really worth and would then bribe the priest of the Temple to allow them to do business. The poor honest people wishing to pay homage to their God were victimized.

Have things changed much from the days of Christ? Would this make you angry? Let's release our imaginations and travel with Jesus into the city of Jerusalem. We shall visit the Temple and find out what drives Jesus to anger.

Meditation

Find a comfortable spot....Let your arms fall at rest....Close your eyes....take a deep breath....Let it out slowly....Whisper, "Jesus."....Relax....

It is a warm spring day....Soft winds blow the desert sands into rising spirals of debris sucked from the desert floor....As Passover nears, the city square is filled with merchants and visitors....Jesus takes a determined stride down the well-traveled road...."Where are we going?" you ask...."To the Temple; it is time to make our sacrifice to God," he answers....A long walk across the thorn-covered roads and the warmth of the noonday sun cause you to question the importance of this trek....As though reading your thoughts, Jesus responds, "I am glad you joined me today. There are things for you to see and hear. Let these things touch your

51

heart."....Passing through the city square, which is bristling with activity, you make your way toward the great Temple.... Jesus quickens his steps as though driven by a power you cannot see....Squawking doves and baying sheep and goats fill the plaza....Roughly hewn pushcarts and stalls are crowded together around the Temple steps....

The moneychangers turn away as you and Jesus pass by.... Two steps at a time, Jesus mounts the stairs....You feel the heavy pounding of your heart as you attempt to keep in Jesus' stride....From the top of the high stairs, the activity taking place around the Temple grounds unfolds....Men dressed in turbans and long flowing garments shout for all to hear.... "Goats for sale, a perfect animal for our Lord."....Grubby hands exchange golden coins of Rome from the callused and weathered hands of the poor, promising good fortune....For a moment it reminds you of the carnival midway with hawkers peddling their wares....

Jesus, his face red with rage, pounds his fist against the great Temple pillars....The force of his wrath causes the walk beneath your feet to crack and crumble away....For this is no ordinary man....Jesus glances toward you, shocked at the fear on your face...."My child," he speaks firmly, "come here! Look about you. What do you see?" (*Pause briefly.*) A small child, clothed only in dirt and rags, pulls at your clothing, begging for food. Tears of hunger and a swollen belly tell his story....The crippled beggar kneels before the Temple steps. In disgust and embarrassment the rich merchants spew on him with spittle....A moneychanger laughingly wrestles a woman's small bag of coins from her grasp....Jesus cries, tears stinging his contorted face...."I cannot watch injustice and do nothing. There is no room in my Father's house for such as this! Go quickly and gather pieces of rope from the animal stalls."....

Jesus takes the rope from your hands and quickly weaves it into a long whip with brutal barbed ends...."Stay here, friend. I must clean my Father's house."....With the fury of a hurricane, Jesus thrashes out against the wrongdoers again and again, sending the animals scurrying to freedom....The rope sings its cruel whistle against the wind....Golden coins fall to the ground only to be eaten by the goats....You stand beneath the branches of a tree....For this is a Jesus you did not know.... You have always pictured a smiling face, love-filled eyes, and children gathered around his feet....The animals are gone, the pushcarts and stalls in disarray....A quiet fills the air....Jesus has cleared the Temple....You tremble in fear at this unknown Jesus. The Jewish leaders gather in small groups of angry-tongued men....

Jesus sighs heavily and slides down the trunk of the tree. Sitting on grass he leans against its gnarled trunk...."Child, do not be afraid"....Patting the ground, he motions for you to sit next to him...."My Father's house is no longer a marketplace and the hungry shall be fed. Do not fear me, for I love you. I banished these people because they do not live according to God's laws. It is not always enough to talk about injustice. There are times that you must take a stand for what it right. Silence is not golden; it is only an escape....Your eyes are for seeing truth, not for looking away."....Jesus wipes a tear from his cheek and places his hand on top of yours....His sweaty palm and heaving chest tell you of the agony of his decision.... Draw a cloth from your pocket and wipe his forehead....Jesus smiles faintly and takes a deep breath...."My friend, are there situations in your own life when you have turned away rather than try to change? Is there someone in your school whom everyone makes fun of? Do you and your friends laugh at your parents and their rules? Is there a person who always eats lunch alone? Do you know why? Is it cool to always go along with the crowd? Talk to me, my child" (*Pause.*)

I will leave you for a moment so that you may speak with Jesus.

Prayer

Heavenly Father, open my eyes and my heart that I may see the world's cruelties and the pain of injustice. Let me move beyond seeing; move me to action that will better the situation. Let my heart feel the pain of hunger, the agony of being homeless, the conflict of parents trying to do the right thing. Let me feel, for a moment, your pain. I pray that I may become part of the solution rather than just another problem. Amen.

As the sun lowers itself below the housetops, it is time for you to leave. Tell Jesus goodbye for now. Carry his message in your heart. Walk down the cobblestone path, open your eyes and return to this room.

Discussion

In the large group of teens, discuss the following questions. Attempt to encourage a response from each student. The more discussion on these points, the better.

- Jesus stuck up for those who were poor and oppressed. Who are the poor and the oppressed in our world today?

- If this were your first encounter with Jesus, how would you feel now?

- What is most likely to stir you into action against injustice?

- What are you going to do to help alter an injustice?

Wells of Hope

Scripture: Jn 4:5-15,19-30
Feast: Third Sunday of Lent (A)
Suggested Music: *Dream Journey*

Have you ever been surprised by the kindness of a stranger? What happened? Was this a person with whom you would normally hang out?

Not long ago I found myself lost in a very poor neighborhood of Portland, Oregon. The sun was quickly leaving the city's horizon, being replaced with glowing neon lights and "Closed" signs. The city streets were littered with empty wine bottles, crushed cigarette butts, and broken dreams. My big white car did nothing to hide me from the ravages of the city. I was sincerely fearful as drunken men and homeless souls held out their hands for the few cents I held in my purse. Feeling hopelessly lost and terrified of my plight, I was startled to the point of tears when a fist pounded on my car top. I was afraid to look out the window and see my fate. The pounding was relentless. A women's voice called out, "Honey, git your white tail out of here. This place ain't safe for your kind." Without waiting for my stammered response, the middle-aged woman, dressed in a ragged but clean top coat, continued, "Go down two blocks, turn right, and then drive straight out of here. God bless!" I have asked myself many times if I would have stopped for her if the positions had been reversed. I hope so. I believe that God sends these messengers of faith into our lives. Perhaps they serve as a wake-up call to remind us that regardless of a person's appearance or ethnic background, God's love falls upon everyone.

In the days of Jesus, the Samaritans were the despised, falling to the level of dogs. Samaritans were half Jewish and half Assyrian, the conquering heroes of the battle for the northern Jewish kingdom. Some stayed and married Jewish women to live in the country of Samaria. They were considered "half-breeds," being neither Jews nor Assyrians. Jews and Samaritans rarely even spoke to each other, fearing the wrath of their communities. Women were on an even lower level of acceptance, with Jewish men thanking God in their prayers that they were not born as a lowly woman. Rabbis debated if women indeed had souls. Would Jesus find this an acceptable behavior?

Jesus made every effort to break down this wall of prejudice based on lack of knowledge and love of fellow man—and woman. There was a time when he broke all the social rules to give a Samaritan woman the gift of living water. Let's release our imaginations to find ourselves near a village in Samaria. The town well lies slightly ahead.

Meditation

Find a comfortable position....Close your eyes....Allow your arms and legs to relax....The sounds around you fade away.... Take a deep breath....Let it out slowly....Whisper, "Jesus.".... Find the calm in the center of your being....

The summer sun lies mid-way in the blue sky above....The warm rays of light nearly blind your eyes....The long walk across the desert lands have caused your throat and mouth to dry....Your lips are blistered and peeling....Children play in the town square with a large ball made of goatskin as their target....The ball sails through the air, landing at your feet.... Kick the ball....Send it flying through the dusty air.... Perspiration pours down your face....Water—you must have a drink from the village well....All you can think about is a cool, refreshing drink of water....

Quickly make your way down the winding path to the well.... You can almost taste the water....A lone man sits by the side of the well....To your surprise it is Jesus!....He looks toward you and says, "There is no dipper for the water. Come and wait with me; someone will come along soon and give us a drink."....Jesus points toward the ball resting center stage among the children, "I had a ball like that when I was a boy," Jesus recollects fondly....Your eyes meet....For a minute it is as though he can look deep inside you....Jesus walks toward the ball, then sends it high into the air....A cloud of dust billows about his sandaled feet....

You grow tired of sitting in the hot sun....Your mouth feels as though it is filled with cotton balls which absorb any moisture remaining within you....Jesus places his hand upon your shoulder...."Relax. There is no need to look for a dipper. Someone is coming this way soon."....

At long last, when you are about to give up on ever getting a drink of water, a woman from the village appears by the side of the well.

Jesus speaks to the woman, an uncommon act of the day. "Would you be so kind to give us a drink from the well?"....
The young woman with long black curls stands with her mouth open in shock...."You are a Jew. Why do you ask me, a Samaritan woman, for a drink?"....Setting down her bucket, she continues, "No one the likes of you has ever spoken to me, let alone ask for my help." Jesus startles her once again by answering, "If you knew who I was, you would ask me to give you living water so you would never thirst again."....
"Living water?" the woman mutters, lowering her bucket into the well...."Does your friend want a drink also?" she asks, looking your way....Nod your head "yes," quickly. Jesus stands now, adjusting the rope belted around his waist. "Anyone who drinks from this well will be thirsty again. If you only knew what a wonderful gift God has for you and who I am, you would ask me for some living water!" The woman's dark eyes widen, "But you don't have a rope or a bucket," she says flatly. "Where do you expect to get this *living* water?"....
Placing his hand upon the edge of the bucket, he continues,

"The water I offer will become a constant spring within, watering you forever with eternal life, never to thirst again."

The woman slowly fills a cup from her wooden bucket.... Carefully studying Jesus, she says, "You sound like you are pretty important. Who are you? Are you a prophet?" Jesus shakes his head slightly, brushing his hair aside....A summer wind sends twisting coils of sandy earth twirling across the courtyard....Jesus sips the cool water from the cup, then, handing the cup to you, he smiles and gestures for you and the woman to sit down with him....You place your back against the ancient well, sipping on its harvest: fresh cool water....The woman stands firm. "Please sir," she says. "Give me some of that water! I will never need to make this long trip to the well again." Jesus tells her, "Go and get your husband."....The woman responds quickly, "But I am not married." Jesus looks deep within her being, "All too true! You have had five husbands and you are not even married to the man you are living with now." The woman lets out a gasp, placing a hand over her mouth....Then stuttering she answers, "You are a prophet! What is your name?" she demands. Jesus takes the hands of the woman, inviting her once again to sit down....Reluctantly she lowers herself to the ground; a large flat rock becomes her seat....Jesus takes the empty cup from your hand and fills it from the woman's bucket....

Jesus speaks to the woman of many things about her past, but never condemning....Placing one hand on her shoulder, he shares his words of wisdom: "Do not take the time to wonder why I have chosen to speak to you. Remember instead that it is not important *where* you worship or how you look that counts but rather *how* you worship that matters. Pray with an honest heart."

Leaving the woman to ponder on this he takes your hands within his, asking, "Do you kneel in church, your head bowed in prayer, but resenting the time it takes from your day? Do you wonder if anyone will guess that your mind is on everything *but* God? Do you reach within your sleeping soul and ask the Holy Spirit to awaken your sense of God? Let me help you, my child." Jesus speaks softly. I will leave you in the quiet of the day for a few moments. (*Pause.*)

The woman stands once again. "Well, at least I know that the Messiah will come and when he does he will explain everything to us."....Jesus, still holding your hand, announces, "I am the Messiah. If the living waters work through you, you will grow to understand that it should not matter what color a person's skin is or where he or she calls home....The waters from this well will fill your soul with joy and thanksgiving. Within these living waters there is hope for everyone and there is love for each of God's children. Take moments of your day and invest them in worshiping God. Give thanks for his blessings. Remember to return to this well of hope, this well of God's wonder."

The sun is beginning to set....Long fingers of darkness criss-cross the courtyard....Jesus stands, "It is time for both of you to return home."....The woman gathers her water jug. Jesus gives her a hug, then waves as she disappears down the road...."She will lead many others to believe in me and the importance of not only living a good life but also of worshiping the Father God, seeking the truth of living water." Jesus places his hands on your shoulders and, calling you by name, he asks, "Will you be able to lead others to believe in me?" I will leave you for a moment so that you can speak to Jesus. (*Pause until they grow restless.*)

Prayer

Jesus, may your Holy Spirit fill me with the faith to come before Father God with honesty and hope. I have often turned my back on those different from myself. May I see your reflection in the eyes of everyone I meet to remind me of your presence in all that I do and see. Amen.

Tell Jesus goodbye for now....Walk away slowly....Turn and wave once more....Open your eyes and return to this room.

Discussion

Select several outgoing young people, or, if you know your group well, invite several students to volunteer to pretend that the balance of the class are non-believers. It will be their job to "convince" the others of the truth of Jesus.

• How will you tell someone about Jesus?

Break down into groups of four to six. Ask the students to share their answers to the following questions:

• Who are the people in our society with whom others do not want to associate?

• Is there one particular group of people with whom you find it difficult to break down social barriers? Why?

• How would Jesus relate to those you find offensive?

• Is it difficult for you to find time to pray? What can you do to help your own prayer life? the prayer life of others?

• Share a time or a way that you are most comfortable and most sincere in talking to God.

• Are you ever guilty of being a "pretend" Christian?

Closing Prayer

Dim the lights. Light a candle. Play the background music. Place a large bowl of water and a ladle on the table. Place small paper cups beside the bowl. Ask the students to spend a few minutes in quiet prayer. By example, you may wish to share your own prayer with the group. This will set the tone.

When they have completed their prayers, invite them to come forward, fill their cups with water, sign themselves, and offer this prayer:

I, [name], drink from the living water of Christ, my Lord.

Close with a group Our Father.

The Prodigal Son

Scripture: Lk 15:11-32
Feast: Fourth Sunday of Lent (C)
Suggested Music: *The Sea* **or "Pardon Your People"/***Gentle***
   Sounds

Have you ever taken a wrong turn in the road and become so lost you didn't know north from south? Perhaps you started a new school or job and there you were in unfamiliar territory. Have any of you ever run away from home? Do you remember why you ran away from home? Was it great at first? What happened when you returned home? Did you stop to think how your parents may have felt while you were gone? (*Keep in mind any particular family situations you may know about.*)

Returning home is not always an easy thing even though it may be the right thing to do. Being lost or running away from the people in our lives is not much different than doing something wrong that separates us from God. Pretty soon we might take the attitude of "What's the difference? God doesn't want me back anyway." In most cases the easiest way back home is to simply say, "I'm sorry."

Jesus spoke often about God's love and forgiveness. One day Jesus told a story about a kind and loving father who had two sons. Jesus wanted to help us understand what God's forgiveness is like. Let's release our imaginations to sit beside Jesus and listen to his words.

Meditation

Find a comfortable spot....Relax your neck muscles; roll your head from side to side....Allow your arms to fall at rest....Close your eyes....Take a deep breath....Let it out slowly....Whisper, "Jesus."....Relax....

You are sitting on the edge of an old wooden dock....Dangle your feet in the cool water....In the distance sea gulls screech, announcing the arrival of fishing boats from the sea....Swarms of tiny minnows swim in circles beneath the dock....

The sun wraps the day in its warm rays....A group of small children play nearby....A hand touches your shoulder....Look up....Jesus smiles warmly, inviting you to join him in the shade of an old gnarled tree on the hillside....Jesus lowers himself to the grassy knoll, motioning for you to join him....Then he begins his story.

"There once was a father who had two sons. The younger one came to the father asking, 'Father, I want you to take an accounting of all your properties and wealth and then give me all of my share now. I am going to the city to live as I want.' Reluctantly, the father divided what he had between the two sons. The father knew that he would miss his son and worried that harm and bad judgment would invade his life.

"The younger son spent his fortune quickly and did many foolish things. He bought his friends, offering food, drink, money, and drugs. It was one party after another until there could be no more parties, and no more friends....The money bag was empty....Finding that he had no place to stay and no money to buy the simplest of meals, he went to work for a pig farmer. Pigs are regarded as unclean, the lowliest of the low animals. It was much like it would be for you to accept a job cleaning restrooms and floors all day, only eating what others had thrown into the dumpsters. The boy became so hungry that he began to eat the pigs' food. Smelly pig squalor oozed between his toes; broken and dried ears of corn were the only food. Life was a far cry from the life he had known as a boy. 'My father's servants lead a better life than I do!' he lamented.

As time passed and reality became harsher, the son was forced to make a decision. 'I will tell my father that I am sorry and hope that he will forgive me. I will offer to work as one of his servants if he will have me.'

"The father stood on a hillside looking toward the long road to the city, longing for his son's return. At last he saw his son walking down the pathway, broken, dirty, and filled with despair. The father ran to greet his son, pulling him to his feet where he had fallen. The son begged for forgiveness. 'We will have a real party and celebrate your return,' the father told his son. Upon their return to the house the older brother was not thrilled over his brother's return. He did not feel that his father should be so quick to forgive his brother's mistakes.

"The father adorned his younger son in a fine robe, a symbol of royalty and a large gold ring set with rubies and pearls, a sign of power and authority. The child of mistakes was not only welcomed back, he was restored to his place within the family," Jesus concludes.

Jesus takes your hand, "God loves you just like the father in that story. Even when you make mistakes and do things that you know you shouldn't, he is always waiting to forgive and welcome you with waiting arms." Jesus stretches his long arms out, showing you how much God loves you....You smile, remembering the days of your childhood when you asked your parents how much they loved you....Jesus chuckles, rubbing your back with the palm of his hand.

"Remember, friend, God's love has no strings attached....All you have to do is open the door to your heart....God loves you just the way you are; asking forgiveness is all you have to do....I know that at times it is hard to even admit our mistakes to ourselves, and harder to recognize our actions as mistakes....Think of those times you ran away from God....Is it hard to say 'I'm sorry?'....How can I help you?" he asks.

I will leave you alone for a while with Jesus. Tell him those things known only to your heart. Give God a chance to welcome you back. (*Pause until group becomes restless, approximately sixty to ninety seconds.*)

Prayer

Heavenly Father, help me to recognize those times I need to say "I'm sorry." May I be able to offer forgiveness to those people in my life whom I hold in anger. Remind me that you have accepted me with all of my faults and errors. I am sorry, my God. Amen.

Discussion

In groups of four to six, share the answers to each questions, one at a time.

- From your own background and experience, with whom do you most closely identify in this story? Why?

- Have there been times in your life when you knew that you should tell someone that you were sorry but the words failed you? Why?

- What is Christ's lesson for you in this story?

Activity

Ask each group to put the parable into a modern setting and then act it out for the others. Each drama should come from the angle of each one of the main characters in the story.

Rise — Walk Beside Me

Scripture: John 11:1-44
Feast: Fifth Sunday of Lent (B)
**Suggested Music: *Dream Journey* or "When You Seek
    Me"/*Gentle Sounds***

What emotions do you feel when I bring up the subject of
death? Uneasy? Sad? Have you attended a funeral that deeply
affected you?

The loss of a person that you love leaves in death's wake an
emptiness and feelings of abandonment. I can feel tears
burning at the back of my eyes when I think of the loss of my
daughter. The death of a pet will bring strong emotion to most
people. We have a tendency to think that death always
happens to someone else, but not to us.

Do you think that Jesus ever cried in sadness? When? One day
Jesus did cry; in fact he sobbed. Most of us think of Jesus as
being strong and having the ability of knowing the outcome of
each situation. Lazarus, the brother of Martha and Mary and a
close friend of Jesus, died suddenly following a short illness.
Jesus did not respond to Lazarus' family's call for help but chose
instead to continue his ministry. "Why?" is the most frequently
asked question concerning this story. Let's release our
imaginations, joining Jesus on the opposite side of the Jordan
River, in the land where John the Baptist once preached.

Meditation

Find a comfortable position....Close your eyes....Feel the
muscles in your arms and legs relax....Take a deep breath....
Let it out slowly; whisper "Jesus."....

You are sitting among the tall blades of grass carpeting the hillside....The sun warms the back of your neck.... Hummingbirds flit from flower to flower, their long beaks reaching deep into the nectar....Children play nearby with a ball made of goatskin....The ball rolls toward you....Kick the ball back to the waiting children....Jesus stands surrounded by people....Some reach out, begging to touch even the hem of his garment....Suddenly, a man bursts through the crowd, carrying a rolled piece of parchment....Take the scroll from the old messenger....Break through the multitude and hand the rolled message to Jesus....Jesus reads out loud, "Please come quickly; our brother Lazarus is near death. Signed, Martha and Mary."....Jesus places the message in the sleeve of his robe and continues ministering to the crowd....

Jesus sees you are worried about Lazarus and whispers, "Lazarus will not die, my friend."....

For two more days you stay by Jesus' side as he reaches out to those in need....Jesus, always compassionate and kind, seems to have forgotten the illness of his friend....During the early evening hours of the second day, Jesus turns to you and announces, "It is time to make our way to the home of Lazarus....He has fallen asleep and I will awaken him."....The disciples prepare for the journey, packing bread and dried fish into knapsacks....There is a great deal of talk among the men, some scolding Jesus with their tone....

Jesus places his hand on your shoulder as you begin the long walk to Bethany....Stones on the pathway cut through the soles of your thin sandals....Jesus seems not to notice....The journey continues in the darkness of night....Jesus walks in silence....Does he know what is to come?....Clouds of dust from the well-traveled road hang heavily in the light of dawn....Beyond the funnels of rising sand, you notice a woman running toward you....The brightness of the early morning sun forms a shroud of light about her shoulders.... She waves her arms frantically....Without looking up Jesus speaks, "It will be Martha."....According to custom, the woman pulls her veil over her face, showing only her

red-rimmed eyes, "Lazarus is dead! He has been in the tomb
for four days!"....The words of anguish are spit out rapidly,
peppered with anger and grief....Martha once again assaults
Jesus with her words, "If you had been here maybe my
brother would still be alive."....

Jesus reaches through her pain, taking her into his loving
arms...."Do not worry. Your brother will live again. I am the
source of all life," he tells her...."But Jesus," you interrupt....
"Trust me," he states firmly....

Although saddened by Lazarus' death, Peter grumbles that his
feet hurt and that his stomach is growling....Joined by friends
of Lazarus, the growing band of people make their way to
Lazarus' tomb....The hillside is filled with large boulders and
barren soil....Nearing the crest of the hill there is a cave
protected with a large stone placed at the entrance. Martha
informs Jesus that the tomb lies ahead, holding within its
boundaries the body of her brother....Many friends and family
have gathered at Lazarus' tomb....Mary, his younger sister,
runs to Jesus' side, pushing you aside....The slim young
woman, bearing a cascade of flowing red hair, breaks into
tears...."Why didn't you come right away?" she cries....Mary
buries her head in her hands and cries in sorrow....

Your eyes sting with tears....Sadness darkens the dawn....
Jesus looks toward you, almost helplessly, then lowering his
head, he breaks into sobs of grief....Tears fall freely down his
bearded cheeks....Even Peter wipes a tear away....John takes
the hand of Martha, leading her to the tomb....Jesus moves
toward a nearby tree....You follow closely behind him....
Leaning on the huge tree trunk, Jesus continues to sob....
Reaching out for the comfort of your love, Jesus takes your
hand in his....Feel his sorrow....Wipe away the tears from his
eyes....Opening your hand, you see a tear drop glistening in
the early morning light....

Jesus gains his composure, joining Martha and Mary....Jesus
motions for you to follow...."Show me where you have laid
him."....You, Jesus, Martha, and Mary approach the tomb of

Lazarus....Jesus commands his disciples, "Take away the stone."....Martha speaks haltingly, "Oh, no, Lord, there will be a bad odor! He has been there for four days."....Jesus apparently does not heed the warning, instructing the men.... "Put your shoulders against the boulder and move it out of the way."....Peter huffs and puffs, his arm muscles straining against the weight of the stone....At last, the stone is rolled free....Jesus, his back turned to you, looks toward the heavens, raising his arms in prayer to his Father. Then he moves closer to the doorway of the tomb and commands, "Lazarus, come out!"....The odor of death permeates the air....You clasp your sweaty hands across your nose.... Everyone stands in silence....You wonder if Jesus has gone too far out on a limb this time, a sentiment that others seem to have....Once more he calls out, "Lazarus, come out here!"....A sound of low grunts, a stirring, comes from within the tomb....Instinct tells you to move away in fear....A few moments later, Lazarus walks from the tomb, his body wrapped in burial cloths....Strips of fraying cloth loosen their hold on death, falling from Lazarus' arms and legs....Lazarus stumbles forward, almost falling upon you....His head is wrapped, his jaws tied shut with a burial cloth beneath his chin and then tied into a knot on top of his head....The crowd moves back in shock and disbelief....Only Martha and Mary rush to embrace Lazarus....Slowly, the crowd moves forward, testing the miracle of death to life....Lazarus stumbles, then falls....Death is still uncertain of life....Shouts of praise ring in your ears...."Lazarus lives!"....

Jesus steps aside and motions for you to follow him, leading you to the shade of the olive tree...."Do not lie in the shadow of doubt, my friend. I did not abandon Lazarus, and I will never abandon you. Lazarus died so that my friends would grow to believe in the glory of God."....Jesus raises his hands in prayer, "Thank you, Father, for hearing my prayer."....He settles down onto the ground near you, leaning the weight of his body against the tree....His eyes are tired; his words are strong....Looking directly into your eyes, Jesus says gently, "I love you as much as I love Lazarus, and I wish to give you new life here on earth and everlasting life in heaven....Martha and Mary asked only that their brother live. I granted their need. If you could ask one thing of me, what would that be?"....Jesus waits for your answer.

I will leave you alone for a few moments to talk to Jesus.

Prayer

Dear Jesus, my heart and mind are filled with my own needs. Give me the judgment to know those that are important and those that are trivial. Grant that I, too, may hear your command to "come forth" in faith and love. Amen.

Discussion

- Jesus did not cry when he was told of Lazarus' death, but he did cry when he went to the tomb. Why? How did you feel when you saw the tears of Jesus?

- What amazes you most about this story?

- Have you ever felt as though God was not listening when you prayed?

- Have you had an experience or a tough decision to make recently that tested your faith?

Activity

Pantomime the Gospel story. Make sure that everyone has a part. Let your imaginations move freely with the dialogue and selection of characters—the crowd of friends, the apostles, four to six people to designate the tomb, one for the large boulder, trees, etc.

Woman Caught in Adultery

Scripture: Jn 7:58-8:11
Feast: Fifth Sunday of Lent (C)
Suggested Music: *Dream Journey*

For most of us it is far easier to condemn a person or action than it is to forgive. This is directly opposite to the way Jesus would like us to be. What is the worst offense that someone could commit? Could you ever forgive the act? Why could you or why could you not forgive? We all know people or situations that hang heavily in our hearts, scars that have never healed. What to do about that is a big question for most of us.

Perhaps this question might explain what I mean. Have you ever been accused of something at home or school and faced punishment for something you didn't do? Was there money missing at work and someone pointed the finger at you? How did you feel?

Jesus was put to the test with this question. Let's release our imaginations, joining Jesus on the Mount of Olives in the Temple courtyard.

Meditation

Find a comfortable position. Tense your body for thirty seconds, then release one part at a time....First your fists, shoulders, back....Now allow your legs to feel limp....Close your eyes....Take a deep breath....Let it out slowly; whisper "Jesus.".....

The dawn is breaking above the hills....Light tickles the treetops, awakening sleeping birds....You yawn and stretch in the new light....A small campfire burns brightly behind you.... Sparks explode sending bursts of fire into the air....Jesus nudges you saying, "Hurry my child; many people are filling the Temple courts. For today more than the sinner shall be on trial here."....Handing you a cup of warm meal and honey he urges you to make yourself ready...."Here they come," Jesus warns....The sobs of a woman make you shudder....She is small with long red hair....She was pretty once....Now she is cold, hungry, and very scared....Rumbling, angry, self-righteous men throw the woman down at Jesus' feet.... Jesus whispers to you, "Jewish law demands death for this woman and if I forgive her they will say I am not following Jewish law. If I condemn her to death the angry men will ask where is all the forgiveness that I preach about....Stand back from the angry crowd, child, and I shall hear their case."

The men of the village surround the woman with a wall of judgment. They say to Jesus, "Master, this woman was caught in the very act of adultery. It is the law that this woman should be stoned."....You gasp, reaching out to help the woman to her feet....Jesus pulls you away asking for only your quiet and compassion....Jesus bends down on his haunches, saying nothing....He starts writing with his finger in the rain-moistened sand....The men, thinking they are being ignored, press Jesus for his answer, struggling to see what he is writing in the sand....Faces blanche....Eyes blink....Some turn away in shame....Jesus rises and says, "That one of you who has never sinned shall throw the first stone."....Then once again, he bends down and writes on the ground....One by one, the men withdraw....Jesus stands alone with the woman still before him....You move to the right of Jesus, watching the scene unfold....

Jesus sits down and looks about him. One by one the angry men have disappeared...."Has no one condemned you?" he asks her....She stands, brushing her tear-stained face with the back of her hand, "No one, sir."....Turning to you, Jesus asks,

"And how do you judge her crime?"....You know that by Jewish law the man also must be punished for the crime of adultery but no names were given and no one came forward....Jesus once against presses you for your judgment.... Whisper your response into Jesus' ear....

Jesus pulls the woman to her feet, wiping the tears from her eyes....He holds her small callused hands in his, "Then I shall not condemn you either. You may go; but do not sin again.".…

The woman walks down the courtyard steps, giving thanks for the forgiveness of Jesus....Jesus turns to you, giving you his full attention, and says, "The woman's life will change. I offered her my forgiveness, just as I offer it to you now.".… Jesus walks down the Temple steps, his arm resting around your shoulders...."I know that it is difficult to avoid some of the world's traps. It is even harder to resist the temptation to take revenge."....Nearing the bottom step, Jesus stops, turning to face you...."I also know that there are people in your life you should forgive. (*Pause.*) Whom do you have trouble forgiving? (*Pause.*) Is it yourself or someone in your life? (*Pause.*) Talk to me, my friend. Let go of those hurt feelings."....

I will leave you alone with Jesus to talk about this. Take your time. (*Pause until they grow restless, sixty to ninety seconds.*)

Prayer

Jesus, I pray that I may be given the grace to leave the judgment of others to God. May I learn the art of forgiveness for my family and friends. There are areas in my own life in which I need help to forgive and love again. May I become a witness for your mercy and love. Amen.

There is much you have learned this day and now it is time to ask for God's blessings and be on your way....Walk toward home....Open your eyes and return to this room.

Discussion

In the large group, invite the students to share their answers to these questions:

- What do you think Jesus wrote in the sand?

- Jesus told the woman, "I will accept you." Do you think that Jesus told her how he would accept her? Did he have guidelines?

- Did he mean he would only accept her if she changed her ways?

- Who accepts you with unconditional love? Family? Friends? No one?

- What or who motivates you to lead a good life?

Ask the group to break into small groups and share answers to the remaining questions:

- What do you do when you really make a big mistake? Do you take responsibility? Withdraw? Become miserable?

- If you could trade places with the woman in the square, what would your emotions be?

- What do you think Jesus would say to you?

- Where do you feel that you have the biggest problem in the area of forgiveness (family, friends, neighbors)? Why?

Closing

Lower lights, play background music, and light a candle. Invite the young people to give private thought to the question, "Where do you feel that you have the biggest problem in the area of forgiveness? Why?"

Invite teens to repeat each line after you from the "Prayer of Sorrow," based on Psalm 51.

Leader: Create a pure heart in me, God,
and put a new and loyal spirit in me.

Do not banish me from your presence;
do not take your holy spirit away from me.
Give me again the joy that comes from your
     forgiveness,
and make my spirit obedient.

Stack your hands together in the center of your group. Say the Our Father together, adding "Thank you, God, for your forgiveness. Amen."

You may want to invite the teens to commit to three or four evenings during the coming week. Each session will be a mini-retreat experience in which they will "walk with" Jesus through his passion and death.

Wash My Soul in Your Love

Scripture: Jn 13:1-17
Feast: The Last Supper (ABC)
Suggested Music: *Bamboo Waterfall* or "I Will Never Forget You"/*Gentle Sounds*

If you knew that this was the last day of your life, with whom would you choose to spend it? How would you choose to spend your time? Where would you choose to be? (*Allow time for discussion.*) Would you take the time to wash the feet of family and friends? Would you take the time to teach a younger brother/sister something they will need to know?

Jesus knew that within less than twenty-four hours he would take his last breath, and yet he chose to spend the last few precious hours of his life with his friends. They sang songs, spoke the words of Scripture, enjoyed each other's fellowship, dined—and then Jesus washed their feet. The washing of feet was a custom of the time. There were no paved roads; shoes usually consisted of sandals, which were open to the desert sands and rock-strewn paths. The lowest ranking servant in a household drew the duty of washing the feet of the guests, and yet Jesus kneeled on the bare wooden floor before each of his guests and gently washed their feet. Why do you think Jesus took this precious time of life to humble himself before his friends?

Perhaps we need to take a few moments to find the answers to this puzzle. Release your imaginations to join Jesus and his friends on a warm spring evening for we too shall feel his gentle touch.

Meditation

Find a comfortable position....Close your eyes....Quiet yourself....Shut out the sounds around you....Take a deep breath....Breath out slowly....Whisper, "Jesus."....

You are sitting around a long table....Women are scurrying about preparing the feast....The smell of fresh baked bread fills the small upstairs room. Roast lamb and small red potatoes are carried in on trays....The light is very dim....The lantern's flickering light bounces off the walls....Jesus looks drawn with a sadness....He reaches up from his position on the floor pillow, taking your hand in his....A faint but loving smile crosses his lips....Judas arrives late, taking his place at the end of the table....John fills the cups with wine from a goatskin flask....Wine dribbles onto the tablecloth....The red stain soaks into the cloth, leaving fingers of red liquid lazily oozing across the table....Peter hands you a goblet made of earthen ware, nodding his head in welcome....

The room is very quiet after Jesus blesses the bread and wine....Jesus places a small piece of the warm golden bread upon your tongue, saying, "Take this and eat it in remembrance of me."....Many of the disciples close their eyes, raising their arms toward heaven, in prayer....You hear footsteps behind you....Quickly glance around....Judas is slipping out the door....No one seems to notice....A look of pain crosses Jesus' face, but he says nothing....He sighs in silent recognition....Within a short time, voices raise and it is as though everyone is talking at once....Each one demands his own time slot in the conversation....

Jesus grasps the edge of the table, pulling himself to his feet....The room falls into silence....He removes his outer garment, takes a towel from a rack and wraps it around his waist, then takes an empty basin and pitcher from the table....Jesus hands you the empty pitcher, "Take this and fill it with water and then bring it to me"....Taking the roughly hewn pitcher from his hand, you quickly make your way down the stairs, through the yard to the well....Pulling the bucket up to the edge of the well, you begin to fill the vessel....You return to the house quickly as the water splashes against the sides of the pitcher, spilling out onto the floor....Jesus takes the pitcher from you...."Thank you, my friend," he says gratefully....

He then hands you a large basin, telling you, "I am going to wash the feet of my disciples," he whispers in your ear....Jesus points to the floor near the feet of James....James stands, placing his hands on the arms of Jesus, "Oh, no, not me Lord! Please call the servant if this must be done." Jesus gently persuades James to take his seat in silence and then motions for you to place the bowl on the wood-planked floor....Water splashes out onto the floor; fingers of water sink into the cracks....You gently direct James's feet into the basin....Jesus bends down on one knee, pouring the water over the feet of James....Then, taking the towel from his waist, he dries the disciple's feet....Tears roll down James's cheeks because Jesus has also washed his soul with God's love....One by one, Jesus leads you around the table washing each man's feet, then drying them tenderly....

At last, it is Peter's turn....Peter stands then moves away from Jesus saying, "Lord, are you going to wash my feet?"....Jesus looks first to you then to Peter explaining, "You do not realize what I am doing, but later you will understand."....Peter takes three large steps backward, his shoulders touching the wall, "You shall never wash my feet."....Jesus walks to Peter's side; speaking firmly he tells him, "Peter, unless I wash you, you will have no part of me."....Peter pulls his feet tightly under the weight of his body...."This is a job for a servant," Peter protests, then reluctantly he removes his sandals and takes a seat on a wobbly wooden bench....You place your hands on his roughly callused feet, lowering them into the bowl.... Particles of sand drift to the top of the bowl....Peter remains silent, feeling shame that Jesus would crouch on the floor in order to wash his feet, the feet of a fisherman.

Jesus now turns to you, taking the bowl from your hand and placing it on the floor...."I am going to wash your feet

now."....Small pebbles and wet grass from the courtyard
tumble to the floor as Jesus removes your sandals....Softly, he
guides your feet into the waiting basin....You shiver as a small
droplet of the cold water splashes onto your leg....Jesus, the
Son of God, the Son of Man, kneels before you....Removing
the towel from around his waist, he gently lifts your feet onto
his lap and wraps the towel around them....The towel is soft
and warm on your feet...."Do you understand what I have
done for you?" he questions his disciples...."And do you, my
friend?" he adds looking into your eyes....He interrupts your
stammered reply, "You call me 'Teacher' and 'Lord,' as you
should, for that is what I am."....Looking around the table at
each man, noticing the absence of one, he shudders, then
continues, "I have washed your feet, as you should wash one
another's feet." Jesus folds the dampened towels automatically
as he speaks, "You should do for others as I have done for you."

The room buzzes with a soft murmur from the confused
men....Jesus takes this time to come to your side....He folds
his legs beneath him, lowering himself onto the floor once
again...."My child, my friend, you will be blessed if you follow
me."....Placing an arm around your shoulders, he whispers, "If
I were to come into your life this very day, this hour, to that place
in your mind and heart, what would you ask that I do for you?
(*Pause briefly.*) Would you ask that I hold you? (*Pause briefly.*)
Would you ask me to forgive your errors?" (*Pause briefly.*)

I will leave you alone with Jesus to answer his questions....
Remain still and quiet....Allow only the voice of Jesus to break
through the wall of silence. (*Pause until they get restless.*)

Prayer

*Lord, wash me clean with the waters of forgiveness. I
take for granted the love and labors of my family. I
put my friends and those I call "friend" to a place of
importance, often forgetting your gentle touch. Guide
me, Lord, that I may follow in your footsteps. Amen.*

It is time to say your goodbyes....It is time to carry this
experience with you....Jesus wraps his arms around you,

sending you out in love....Walk through the door of the upstairs room; walk down the stairs and into this room.

Discussion

In small groups of four take a few moments for each to answer the following questions.

- How has someone you know "washed your feet"?

- With Jesus knowing your every need, how would Jesus "wash" your feet today?

Prayer Service

Bring the group together. Lower the lights, or use candlelight. Play background music. Explain that each will have an opportunity to experience footwashing if he/she wishes. Do not make it mandatory but encourage each to participate. Begin by selecting several young people, wash their feet, and then ask them in turn to wash another's, and they in turn, another. You will need the following items:

- two or three large bowls suitable for footwashing

- two or three pitchers of warm water

- clean towels

In silence allow time for each student to experience "footwashing." Suggest they remain in prayer, thinking about the answer to this question:

- Is there a person in your life who needs a gentle loving touch from you? Perhaps someone in your own home?

As the washing of the feet draws to a close, gather in a large circle. Invite those that wish to volunteer a prayer. Close with praying the Our Father.

Father, I Do Your Will, Not Mine

Scripture: Mk 14:32-42
Feast: The Passion (ABC)
Suggested Music: *Dream Journey* or "Without You, Lord"/*Gentle Sounds*

Have you ever felt as though everyone you knew had abandoned you? As though there were no friends, no family to turn to? What made you feel this way? What made you feel better—time, the action of another, realizing you had to pull it together? Have you ever wondered if Jesus ever felt lonely and sad? When?

There was a night that Jesus felt all the loneliness and sadness that the world could hold. Jesus knew that he was going to be put to death, and, like us, he was afraid. Jesus begged his Father to change his mind. From time to time we have all been asked to do something very difficult. Have you ever had to beg your parents to change their mind? Imagine Jesus' humility in asking his Father to change his mind over the course of Jesus' life. Let's release our imaginations into a time of sadness, a time of grief.

Meditation

Make yourself comfortable....Stretch your arms in the air.... Settle down....Close your eyes....Take a deep breath....Let it out slowly....Whisper, "Jesus."....Relax.

15. Father, I Do Your Will, Not Mine

The Passover meal is over....Jesus leads you and the disciples from the upper room out into the quiet street of Jerusalem.... John moves ahead of the small band, a rusty lantern swinging back and forth on his arm....Light speckles the cobblestone streets....Jesus walks with his head down, sadness shrouding his face....The quiet shuffling of feet is the only sound you hear....The yowling of a cat shatters the silence....Jesus leads you through the gate of the city toward the Garden of Gethsemane....

Jesus hesitates at the gate of the garden...."Wait here while I go into the garden and pray," Jesus announces....Before you can lower yourself onto the grassy knoll, Jesus speaks again, "Peter, John, James, and you, my friend," Jesus says, pointing to you, "please stay with me."....Jesus' shoulders droop, his footsteps are heavy....Jesus reaches out his hand for yours....His touch is gentle....His fingers fold about your hand, not clasping, just holding, enjoying your touch....Jesus wipes a small tear from his eye....Looking directly at you, he explains, "I am feeling very sad tonight. I shall never come here again."....Jesus stops, calling out, "Wait here for me. Do not leave me alone tonight."....

Jesus walks further into the garden, falling onto his knees....His broad shoulders hang heavy as though he carries the weight of the world upon his back....Jesus falls forward, burying his face in the cold, hard ground....Jesus breaks into tears....The sound of sorrow, the sound of loneliness, and the sound of fear fill the night....Jesus' body shakes with the depth of his sobs....Move closer to Jesus....Lie down next to him.... Put your face close to his....Hear his sadness....Touch his hand....Let him know you love him....Touch his sadness.... Jesus begs his Father in heaven, "Father, Father, everything is possible for you. If it is possible, take this cup of sorrow from me." Stillness and acceptance settle over him....Looking to heaven, he speaks again, "Father, I will do your will, not mine."

Jesus slowly raises himself from the ground....Standing in silence, he takes your hand in his once again....Walk down the gentle slope where James, John, and Peter lie sleeping....

Jesus looks at his friends, shaking his head....He whispers his sorrow, "You could not watch with me even one hour."....
Jesus walks away slowly, dropping to his knees....He continues to pray, "If this cup of sorrow cannot pass unless I drink it, your will be done."....Jesus returns to his disciples....
Sadly, he sees they are still fast asleep....He looks at you, his eyes damp with tears. "They do not understand what the night will bring." Jesus kneels in prayer, leaning against a huge boulder; his hands folded, his eyes looking upward, he slowly repeats his pleading, "Father, if possible, let this cup pass from me."....The moonlight casts eerie shadows across the garden....Clouds move across the night sky....

Only you and Jesus remain awake....He moves quietly toward you....His walk is slow....He is standing beside you....His cheeks glisten in the moonlight, wet with tears....Leaning against a tree trunk, Jesus lowers himself to the ground once again....Take your hand and wipe away his tears....Hold his tears in the palm of your hand....Place your hand over your heart, allowing his tears to soak into your clothing....Jesus smiles gently at you and begins to speak, "I must leave you soon. It is my Father's will that I must suffer and die so that mankind will be saved. I must obey my Father."....He turns away from you, walking toward the garden gates....Run down the sloping hillside....Try to catch up with Jesus....No matter how fast you run Jesus is just beyond your reach....His fate is sealed and you must watch it unfold....In the distance you hear angry voices....Burning torches light the sky....Breathless, you are able to walk with Jesus as he faces his enemies. I will give you time to speak to Jesus....

Prayer

Dearest Jesus, I wish I could take away your loneliness and sadness. You have filled my life with hope. Forgive me, Lord, for those times that I have not been willing to obey, not been willing to follow. May your Holy Spirit guide me to follow your example of obedience. Amen.

It is time to leave Jesus....He knows that you walk beside him in this difficult hour....Open your eyes and return to this room.

Discussion

Working in small groups, ask each person to share his/her answer to the following questions:

- If you had a few days to live, what would you do in those days?

- Is it harder for you to *know* what God's will is for you or is it harder for you to *do* God's will?

- Is there a special place where you go when you are facing a difficult situation? Do you want people around you or would you rather be alone?

- Are you facing a hard decision now? Can we help with this decision?

Closing

After the sharing, form a circle of friendship. In oneness and dependence on each other, pray for each other. Close with the Our Father.

The Gift of Forgiveness

Scripture: Mt 26:69-75
Feast: The Passion (ABC)
Suggested Music: *Dream Journey* or "Without You, Lord"/
    Gentle Sounds

Have you ever blown it big time, making the kind of mistake that you never think you can redeem? What does that feel like? Is it like death grown cold? Darkness with no light at the end of the tunnel? Some of us are still waiting for the other shoe to drop. In other words, we know how badly we messed up; it just may not have been discovered yet. But when it is...

Take a minute and think of the men who surrounded Jesus. Is there someone who you think really dropped the ball? Who (Judas, Peter, the woman who committed adultery, the nine lepers)? What did they do or not do? Judas hung himself. Perhaps he could never forgive himself. Only in the moment of death did he realize what he had done. But what about Peter? He had climbed the mountaintop to see Elijah and Moses. Jesus called him "Cephas," the "rock" upon which he would build his church. And yet in the hour of darkness Peter turned his face from our Lord. Was it fear? Shame? Knowing our own pain when we know we have failed the test, do we have any concept of how Peter felt? Let's release our imaginations to go back to the darkness of evening and the blackness of fear.

Meditation

Make yourself comfortable....Take a deep breath....Let it out slowly....Whisper, "Jesus."....Feel your arms relax....Close your eyes and shut out the world around you....

You sit in silence around the long table....Jesus passes the cup to you and smiles sadly....For this is the end....Press the cup to your lips....Smell the sweetness of the grape....Only James breaks the silence...."Join me now in song. Let us raise our voices to our heavenly Father."....The song is sung, but there is no joy. There is no merrymaking; there is only the silence of death's messenger....Jesus sits on his knees; raising his voice gently, he speaks, "This very night you will all fall away because of me, for it is written: 'I will strike the shepherd, and the sheep of the flock will be scattered'"....Your eyes meet Jesus'....You turn away in shame for all those times you have forgotten his name....

Jesus places his hand on your shoulder....not to take away the pain, but to let you know he feels your shame....

Jesus stands, adjusting his robe, "After I have risen, I will go ahead of you into Galilee."....Peter rubs his scruffy beard and quickly proclaims, "Even if all fall away on account of you, I never will."....Only Peter can speak with such conviction....Jesus looks down at the floor, then speaks, "I will tell you the truth. This very night before the rooster crows, you will disown me three times."....Peter makes a fist and slams the table....The cups dance on the uneven wood. "Even if I have to die with you, I will never disown you," he says, once again hitting the table....All the other disciples say the same....You nod your head and look downward....

The meal is finished, the message delivered....You make your way down the dark stairway into the night....No one carries a lantern for fear of being seen....Silently the group follows Jesus to the Garden of Gethsemane....The hour is late and your eyes are filled with heaviness....Although Jesus has asked all of you to stay awake with him, the hour finds you all fast asleep....In the fog of slumber, Judas arrives....There is a large crowd with him armed with swords and clubs....James huddles near you. "The chief priests and elders have sent them to arrest Jesus. Truly, the end is near!" James whispers....Judas kisses Jesus on the cheek and the night has come to an end.... You slide in behind the large boulder where a few moments before Jesus had knelt in prayer...."What can I do?" you ask yourself....

You rise and follow the milling crowd....Jesus, his wrists wrapped with a leather thong, stumbles through the night air....Approaching a large house sitting above the city, Jesus is dragged to Caiaphas, the high priest....Teachers of the law and the elders are assembled, sitting on carved wooden benches, reminding you of our juries and courtrooms....Look behind you....It is Peter....He walks among the guards, pulling his cloak tightly around his head....You find safety behind a group of onlookers....Fear grips your throat....Weakness fills your limbs....The high priest bellows at Jesus, "Are you the Christ, the Son of God?"....Make your way through the crowd, closer to Jesus....Can you hear what he is saying to the elders?....What do you think he is saying? (*Pause briefly.*)

Look around for Peter....Peter, the rock....the head of Christ's church....Peter sits in a crumpled heap in the courtyard....A servant girl passes by Peter, asking, "You were with Jesus of Galilee?"....Peter turns his head away, "I don't know what you are talking about" he states emphatically....

Follow Peter to the gate to ask him what he is going to do.... Before you can catch up with him another girl cuts across the dark courtyard, calling out to the guards, "This fellow was with Jesus of Nazareth."....Peter bustles past you, yelling, "I don't know what you are talking about!"....A small group of the curious block Peter's path....Look directly at Peter....His eyes squint in the darkness of night...."You are one of them!" the crowd rings out...."For the last time, I do not know this man!"....No one notices you....Your silence rings loud in your ears....Immediately in the distance you hear a rooster crow.... Peter falls to his knees remembering Jesus foretold this happening, "Before the rooster crows, you will disown me three times."....Peter grasps your hand and leads you outside....Falling to the ground his body shakes with shame and sorrow....Looking up, taking your face into his rough callused hands, he speaks through his tears, "Child, have you ever felt like this?....As though the world is crushing in all around you?"....Looking upward toward the heavens Peter continues to ask, "How could I have turned my face away from Jesus?"...."What made you claim that you do not know Jesus?" you ask, choking back the tears, knowing the many times you too have acted as though you do not know this man....Peter wipes away the tears with the back of his hand, "Talk costs nothing. I failed because I wasn't as strong as I thought. My faith disappeared. I tell you these things so that you might find forgiveness for yourself. God uses even our failures, my friend."

Jesus is allowed to sit down, his head downcast....His judges, milling about, notice you....They motion for you to join him.... Jesus places his finger on his mouth, "Shhh!"....For he does not want you in danger. Make your way quietly to Jesus' side....

I will leave you alone with Jesus for the end of this long night....For the morrow will bring a closing....Take a few minutes to think of those times you too have turned your back on Jesus....the times that you have failed....Have you ever felt like Peter? Share these things with your Lord....

Prayer

Jesus, I come before you knowing how many times I have failed. Grant that I may be strengthened by these events. Turn the negative into positive, for only you can use failure to make me into the person that God wants me to become. Amen.

It is time to leave Jesus on this sad night....Jesus whispers, "I love you." Turn and walk into the night....Open your eyes and return to this room.

Activity

Break into small groups of four to six.

- Have you ever had an experience similar to Peter's? Perhaps a time of turning your back on friends or family, a time of going your own way regardless of the costs?

- Have you asked for God's forgiveness, or is it too hard to even admit your own mistake?

Prayer Service

Supplies: petri dish, small amount of kitty litter, background music, candle, paper and pencils

In small groups, join in a prayer service for each other in the name of Christ. Each person will be prayed with to overcome a feeling of pain or guilt. One at a time, write down a time of hurt and pain on paper; place the paper into the burning flame. The group then lays hands on the teen in prayer or lets him/her know they care in some other non-verbal way. As each group completes this celebration, close with one verse of "They Will Know We Are Christians by Our Love."

At the close, join together with your arms over the shoulders of each other. In this display of oneness and acceptance, pray for each other. Dismiss quietly when finished.

What Say You?

Scripture: Mk 15:1-15
Feast: The Passion (B)
Suggested Music: *Dream Journey* or "Without You, Lord"/*Gentle Sounds*

For a moment, think back to your childhood to a time when you were punished, justly and unjustly. (*It may help to have a personal illustration ready.*) What childhood punishment do you remember most vividly? Do you believe that you were punished fairly or unfairly? How? At that time did a brother or sister come to your defense or did they make matters worse for you?

Have you ever watched from the sidelines as someone you know got into trouble? Did the person deserve the punishment? Was there anything that you could have done to help but didn't do? Why didn't you come to the person's defense?

Have you ever witnessed a situation in which a brother or sister was punished harshly but you knew he/she was not guilty? What would/could you have done in this case? Did you choose to say nothing rather than possibly incriminate yourself?

If you had the opportunity to have been with Jesus when he was sentenced to die by crucifixion, would you have turned your back and walked away? What would you say in his defense? To whom? After witnessing Jesus' miracles and hearing his words, the crowd now demanded his death. Let us release our imaginations into the fateful evening of Jesus' arrest and find out what our actions might have been.

Meditation

Make yourself comfortable....Close your eyes....Roll your shoulders....Take a deep breath....Let it out slowly....Whisper, "Jesus."....Relax....

It is now the early hours of morning....The night has barely passed....Sun rises slowly from its resting place behind the distant hills....A strange dampness fills the air....Candles flicker, spreading light into the dark halls of the high priest's home, where all of the chief priests and other Jewish leaders have gathered....There is an ill will about the room....The Sanhedrin, the whole Jewish Supreme Court, is trying to find something against Jesus that will be sufficient to condemn him to death....You hide in the shadows, trembling....These men have questioned Jesus repeatedly demanding, "Do you call yourself 'the Son of God?'"....Jesus, speaking softly, answers, "I am, and you will see me sitting at the right hand of God."....The high priest's face reddens, his lips curl in disgust as he tears at Jesus' clothing, leaving Jesus naked to the waist....You turn away, fear and sadness filling your eyes with tears...."Sentence him to death. End this night and his false rule forever," demands a voice from the angry crowd...."If this man is truly the Son of God, let a witness come forward," the high priest calls out....You slide further into the darkness the shadows provide....Do you speak?...Do you remain in silence? (*Pause briefly.*)

Jesus, his hands tied with a leather thong, is led from the room....A decision has been reached to take him to Pilate, the Roman governor....Pilate will decide the fate of the man called Jesus....The road is strewn with rocks....You feel the sharpness of the stones cutting into your thin sandals....Jesus, his head bowed, is dragged through the streets....Throngs of people stand along the roadway....Some turn their heads as he passes by, shame and sadness filling their hearts....Others jeer and taunt, "Hail, the king of the Jews!"....You push your way closer to Jesus, but still you seek the shadows...."What can I do?" you whisper to yourself....The question remains unanswered....

Jesus is dragged into the presence of Pilate. Although he is the governor, he stands only a little over five feet tall....His dark beard is neatly trimmed. Pilate struts his small frame back and forth across the balcony....He seems annoyed with this interruption in his daily routine. For he has often heard of Jesus, fearing a takeover of power....Below in the courtyard, Jesus stands, his clothing nearly torn away....The crowd surrounds Jesus....They jeer and spit at this man, your friend...."Are you the king of the Jews?" Pilate asks in a high-pitched voice...."Yes," Jesus replies. "It is as you say".... Witnesses step forward to falsely accuse Jesus....Jesus remains silent....You close your eyes, not wanting to see....A mob of angry people begins to crowd toward Pilate demanding the release of another prisoner, Barabbas. It was Pilate's custom to release one Jewish prisoner each year at Passover—any person the people requested....In frustration, Pilate calls out, "If I release Barabbas, what shall I do with this man you call your king?"....The sound of the crowd will forever ring in your ears, "Crucify him!" they scream....A burly hand reaches forward, grabbing at Jesus' tattered robe....The little man with so much power calls out, "But why? What has he done wrong?"....The crowd roars louder than ever, "Crucify him!"....Beads of perspiration form on Pilate's forehead. He fears the crowd will turn on him....The multitude has become wild and demanding....A stocky little man pushes from behind, nearly knocking you to your feet....He spits in the face of Jesus....Jesus remains calm, accepting his fate....Looking at the little man you recognize him. He once stood at Lazarus' tomb when Jesus called Lazarus from the dead...."Why then can this man, who has seen the miracles and heard the word, turn against Jesus?" you ask no one in particular....Jesus turns his head slightly, catching sight of you from your place of shadows. "My child, where have you been?" he asks...."How can these people who know you so well turn their back on you now?" you ask....Jesus looks down, a tear forming on his cheek...."Have you never turned away from me?" (*Pause briefly.*) "I love you. I must do this for you. It is not always enough to call yourself 'Christian,' for you must *be a*

Christian." Jesus looks into your eyes. Reaching out for your hand, he asks, "In the hours of days past have you not turned your back to me also?" The crowd stands frozen in a moment of time as you are given a chance to answer Jesus. (*Pause.*)

Once again amid the catcalls bellows a voice from across the crowd, "Are you the King of the Jews?"....Jesus stands before them, his head held high, his eyes transfixed....as though he has entered into another place, another time....Pilate has ordered Jesus flogged with a leaded whip....The Roman soldiers place a purple robe across Jesus' shoulders, mocking him with this sign of royalty....A crown of long, sharp thorns is placed on his head....They push the crown onto his head.... Droplets of blood stain Jesus' wounded face....The soldiers take turns saluting Jesus, yelling, "King of the Jews!"....They beat him on the head with a cane, pushing the thorns deep within his flesh....But he speaks not to his tormentors. Jesus turns once more toward you, speaking in a whispered voice, "I love you my child."....Jesus is led away to be crucified....

Prayer

Dear Jesus, I am sorry for hiding in the shadows of my life. I know that my mistakes have separated the two of us. You took this punishment for me. Please forgive me for being weak. Strengthen my life with your Holy Spirit so that I may learn to serve you and your people. Amen.

Jesus is led away to be crucified....You kneel as he passes....A warm glow fills your body....Sunlight peaks through the clouds....Say goodbye to Jesus....Open your eyes and return to this room.

Discussion

Form small groups. Allow time for everyone to answer each individual question. There are no right or wrong answers.

- Why did Jesus go through this torture when he could have called it off at any time? How does this make you feel?

17. What Say You?

- Pilate probably did not want to crucify Jesus, but the crowd demanded and Pilate caved in to pressure. Have you ever caved in to the pressure of a "crowd"? Will you do anything to keep the peace and be part of the crowd?

- If you were on trial for being a follower of Jesus, would you be convicted or set free? Why?

Standing in a circle with hands clasped, close with the Our Father.

Forgive Them, Father

Scripture: Mk 15:21-40
Feast: The Passion (B)
Suggested Music: *Thunderstorms* or *Dream Journey* or "Without You, Lord"/*Gentle Sounds*

If I were to ask you to share what you think to be the most significant part of the crucifixion, what would you tell us? Why? For some it is when the nails are driven into Jesus' wrists and feet—hearing the sound of the heavy mallet tearing through flesh, the crunching of bone, the beginning of the final agony. Visualize how he must have gasped for breath, biting his lips until they bled. What is the hardest part of Jesus' death and crucifixion for you to understand? Does the crucifixion and death of Jesus affect you personally? Why? Why not?

When I think of the pain Jesus endured I have to put it in my own perspective of agony. I only know personally of one pain that might compare. It brings my thoughts to the day my daughter died. Upon learning of her death in a cold, sterile operating room, I let out a cry—a wild sound that came from deep within. There is no cry so deep, so unbelieving, so devoid of hope to compare with this. This scene reminds me of the pain that God suffered during the crucifixion. He could have relieved his son of this burden but chose instead to allow Christ's death to save mankind. Could any of us send our child to a painful death? I think not.

Has there ever been a death of a family member or friend that has affected your life? How?

Most of us spend the rest of the church year thinking about anything and everything but this moment in time. We know about it but we do not know it in a personal way. Let's release our imaginations to travel to Golgotha and the day that changed the world forever.

Meditation

Make yourself comfortable....Close your eyes....Move away in spirit from the people near you....Let your arms relax, hanging loosely at your side....Your legs are limp....Take a deep breath....Let it out slowly....Whisper, "Jesus."....

It is early morning....The night has been long....You stand on a rock-strewn hillside....The cries of the dying fill the air....One by one the bodies are removed from crucifixes....The thieves and murderers are hung to die in this barren place of death.... The odor of death hangs heavily in the morning sun....Jesus is making his way up the path to his own execution....The crowd jeers and taunts him with every final step he takes....His mother, Mary, and his friends follow behind this parade of death....

Jesus falls for the third time....His legs are bruised....Sweat pours down his face, mixing with his blood....His tattered garment is nearly gone....As he falls this third time his head turns toward you....His eyes dart through the reality of pain to notice you....He reaches toward you but the sting of a Roman whip slices through the morning mist....Jesus balances the 125-pound crossbeam across his shoulder and attempts to rise under its weight....Simon of Cyrene, drafted into sharing the weight of the beam, grimaces as the beam cuts into his shoulder....It is clear he does not want to share this burden with Jesus....Simon notices Jesus glancing your way and asks you, "Why do you not offer to help? He is your friend, not mine." (*Pause.*)

Dirt from the road and spittle from his enemies coat Jesus' body and clothing....There is one other sound carried on this morning's misery....Soft wails of suffering and loss....Women gather, unafraid to show their mourning....Women who remember his words....Women who danced at the wedding in Cana....Women who watched as the daughter of a Roman soldier rose from her deathbed....Women of Galilee....Women weep the tears of agony....John reaches out to comfort the mother of Jesus....You are so close to her that you feel her anguish, her body convulsed in pain....At long last Jesus reaches the top of the hill....It is almost over....The crowd is angry....They push to the front of the pack....They all want one more chance to show their disgust....

It is nearly noon....The sun moves endlessly on, retracing its steps across the sky....Clouds are dancing on the wind....The heavy, rugged crossbeam is torn from Jesus' grasp and thrown upon the ground....Wine drugged with bitter herbs to deaden the pains of death are offered to him, but he refuses it....The Roman captain of the guard shoves you out of the way....Those of you who dare follow Jesus this far are tossed aside like fabric dolls....Some of his followers hide from sight for fear of their own end....Jesus is thrown to the ground and placed upon the tree of death....Jesus lies motionless upon his cross, glancing to the heavens for the grace to die....Soldiers stand guard holding the crowd at a distance....Two solders, not much older than you, are given large mallets, several times larger than hammers that you know....A discussion is taking place between the captains and the men armed with mallets.... They do not want him to die too quickly....Fearing that the nails will tear his flesh apart if they put the nails into his palms, causing his body to fall to the ground, they decide that the nails must enter his wrists to provide an anchor of sorts....You shudder in sorrow....

You shudder in horror....

The first hammer is swung, hitting the nail sharply....The loud sound of metal hitting metal echoes through the now silent crowd....Mary lays her head upon John's shoulder, weeping softly....Place your hand upon her back....Allow her to feel your love....Blood spurts up into the air, a geyser of life-filled liquid, falling sharply upon the ground only to turn to death.... A sharp cracking of bones crackles in your ears....Over and over again, the solders pound the nails until at last the deed is accomplished....Jesus bites into his own lips in pain, looking to the heavens for release from his earthly body....He gasps in pain as the cross is lifted upright, his full weight pulling on the nails....He gasps again, he can inhale but cannot exhale with his arms outstretched....A small sign is nailed to the cross.... "The King of the Jews"....

Roman solders kneel beneath the cross, gambling for the cape of Jesus....You wonder if the winner's life will be changed with this turn of luck....Two robbers are also crucified on this morning, their crosses on either side of Jesus....The crowd passes beneath the cross jeering at him as they walk by. "Ha! Look at you now!" they yell at him. "If you are truly the Son of God, come down from the cross and save yourself."....You look upward into his pain-contorted face, offering your love as the only solace....A chief priest stands near the foot of the cross, taunting, "You are clever at 'saving others,' they say, but you can't save yourself!"....Even the two robbers dying with him curse him....You grab a sponge and dip it into a bucket and raise it upon the end of a stick, but Jesus, knowing the end is near, turns his head away....

Rays of sunlight warm the back of your neck and arms.... Suddenly without warning, darkness covers the entire land.... There is a deep rumbling from the clouds....The wind whistles through your hair....It is noon, and death is taking its last breaths....You fall back in fear for the heavens are bursting open with rain and wind....For three hours you sit huddled near Mary, the mother of Jesus....Mary Magdalene and other Galilean women who are his followers call out to you, "My child, he dies for us."....You fall to the ground in remorse for all the times that you have forgotten him....for all the times you turned away from him....Your words remain unspoken.... Jesus knowing your heart nods his head upon his chest....Take a moment to talk with him before death covers the land. (*Pause*.)

Thunder shakes the earth....The darkened sky is now devoid of light....It is three o'clock in the afternoon....For three hours you have watched his relentless suffering, wondering when

God would end the pain....Then Jesus calls out with a loud voice, "My God, my God, why have you deserted me?"....At last Jesus utters another loud cry, one from deep within his body....A cry so loud and piercing that it could be an animal injured in the wild....You will forever hear the sound....It is the cry of death....Jesus dismisses his spirit....Life turns to death....A Roman officer standing beside his cross sees how Jesus dismissed his spirit, and cries out, "Truly, this is the son of God!"....Mary screams the cry of a mother....a cry that death has taken her son, her baby....

Prayer

Dear Jesus, I fall to my knees before you. You alone are my Lord, my Messiah. Never let me forget again what you have done for me. You have been punished for crimes that are not yours. My sins have added to your burden. Amen.

The day has drawn to a close....Mary sits at the base of the cross holding the body of her son....She weeps silently, rocking back and forth as though she were still holding the infant Jesus....John approaches you, wiping a tear from your cheek and looking toward Mary. "The child in each of us always belongs to our mother."....The words to a Christmas carol run through your mind...."What Child Is This?"....His body, now lifeless, hangs like a limp doll in the arms of his mother....Reach forward and take his limp hand into yours.... Hold it for a moment....There is no life within this body. However, as you hold his hand, a warmth goes through you and you know he shall walk this earth again....There is hope, for this is a beginning, not an ending. It is time for you to leave....Rise and walk away....Open your eyes and return to this room....

Allow the group to sit in silence for a few moments, with the lights dimmed.

Prayer Service

Dim the lights. Place a cross, lighted by candlelight or a small spotlight, in a place of honor and reverence. Continue to play the music from Thunderstorms. *Play for one minute, then return to original music choice of either* Dream Journey *or "Without You, Lord"/*Gentle Sounds.

Read aloud Isaiah 53:2-6. Allow a few moments of silence. Invite those who wish to share their feelings. Stress that you want them to be honest and there are no wrong answers. If the group needs more stimulus ask each one to share, "The crucifixion of Jesus makes me feel...because...."

At the close, gather together in a circle holding hands. Pray the Our Father. Dismiss quietly.

A New Dawn

Scripture: Mt 28:1-10; Mk 16:1-8; Lk 24:1-11
Feast: Easter (ABC)
Suggested Music: *Dream Journey* or "We Believe in You"/*Gentle Sounds*

Within the pages of Scripture, we find that God chooses the most unlikely people for his messengers. Start with Peter. What stories of Peter come to mind? He was rough and crude, impatient with others. He lived to deny knowing Jesus three times that we know of, and yet Jesus built his church upon this crudely cut rock. In the call of the fishermen none of these men was well educated. They certainly did not have any "good connections," no social status; they may not have been able to write their own names. They probably did not even understand what Jesus was talking about most of the time. Does this give us hope? I think so! Are there other messengers you can think of whom you would never have chosen (e.g., Mary Magdalene, the woman at the well, Nicodemus, Paul, the tax collector, Zacchaeus)?

I often wonder what my reaction would have been had I found the tomb empty and a young man dressed in brilliant white clothing sitting beside the empty tomb, telling me that Jesus had risen. Oh, sure, I would have bought that one real quick. (*Invite discussion.*) Would you have believed? Would someone have had to prove it to you? Or would you have come to a logical conclusion that someone stole the body of Jesus? How would you feel in finding the empty tomb?

If these events were to happen today, what type of person would Christ choose to be the first one in the empty tomb?

Let's relive that morning in our imaginations.

Meditation

Make yourself comfortable....Close your eyes....Shut out the world around you....Feel your body relax....Take a deep breath....Let it out slowly....Whisper, "Jesus."....

It is early morning on the third day following Jesus' death.... The sun is just rising above the rooftops....Roosters signal the beginning of day: "Cock-a-doodle-do."....The women who followed Jesus from Galilee are walking to the tomb to anoint his body with oils. Mary of Magdala notices you and invites you to join them....Grab a jacket....The early morning air is chilly....Mary hands you a bottle of oil....Walk slowly up the steep hillside....Be careful not to spill the oil....One of the women asks, "Who will move the big stone away from the entrance to the tomb so that we can go inside?"....

After some time you arrive at the top of the grass-covered hill....Overnight, flowers have blossomed....Red tulips, yellow daisies, and white lilies wave their heads in the gentle breeze....Butterflies flit from flower to flower....You have never seen so many butterflies....Look to the right....There is Jesus' tomb....The stone is rolled back. "Who has done this?" questions one of the women....Mary motions for you to join.... "Let's look inside," she suggests....One cautious step at a time, you and Mary step through the doorway of the tomb.... A chill goes down your spine....It's empty!....Nothing remains except for the burial cloths....Strips of white woven cloth lie scattered at your feet....You hear a stirring from the doorway of the tomb....A bright light shines, dazzling your eyes....A young man, dressed entirely in white, speaks to you...."Why are you looking in a tomb for someone who is alive? He isn't here! Jesus is not dead!" The angel slowly rises to his feet.... "Remember, he told you that he would be handed over to people who would crucify him, but on the third day he would rise from the dead....Jesus has been raised up."....Not

101

understanding this, Mary begins to cry, "They have taken Jesus away."

Three of the women run off down the hillside toward Jerusalem...."They are going to tell everyone that the body of Jesus has disappeared," Mary explains....You and Mary walk over to a large olive tree....You sit beneath its huge branches....Mary cries softly....She turns around and notices a man standing beside her....You are startled and let out a gasp of fear....The man speaks softly, "Why are you crying? Whom are you looking for?" he asks. "Where is Jesus?" Mary demands....Gently, the man touches Mary's shoulder, whispering, "Mary!"....Mary, wiping her tears away, stares intensely at the man....She cries out, "It is Jesus!"....You turn rapidly to study this man....He smiles slightly, calling your name, "Did you too think that I had left you?" he asks....It really is Jesus! His body can no longer rest in the tomb, for he is alive!...."My child, I have chosen you to carry my message to others."...."Why me?" you stutter, your mind swirling with questions and fear....You step forward into his open arms.... Jesus is alive!

The soft blades of grass on the hilltop and new blossoms bursting through petals of green are testimony to life.... Breathe in the sweet fragrance of flowers....Mary gathers the other women about her, talking excitedly....She runs down the hill to tell the others about Jesus....God brought his son, Jesus, back to life!

You stand alone with Jesus in this beautiful place....The sun shines warmly now....Jesus holds out his loving arms to you once again....Feel his arms wrap around you...."I will always keep my promises to you. Are there times when you doubt my presence in your life?" he whispers in your ear. (*Pause.*) Imagine that you are very small....Climb up onto his lap....Feel his love and protection. Take this time to talk to Jesus.... Speak to him from your heart. I will leave you alone with Jesus.

Prayer

Dear Jesus, through my imagination I witnessed the events of Easter morning when you rose from the dead to a new life. Through you I will have life everlasting. Help me to live my life with this hope. May your Spirit strengthen me so that I may be a good witness in the world to all that you did and said. Amen.

It is time to leave Jesus....Tell him goodbye for now....Rise and walk down the sloping hillside....Open your eyes and return to this room.

Prayer Service

The lights should remain low or use the light of candles. Prepare a table for an agape with bread and wine or grape juice, if you prefer.

Gather together, encircling the table. Sing a familiar song of celebration. Then ask each person to come to the table, breaking off a piece of bread and taking a sip of the grape juice or wine, repeating, "Jesus is with us!"

All who wish may share their thoughts with the group. Invite the teens to pass the sign of peace, "May the Lord be with you, [name]," among the group members.

Ask for prayer intentions and have the teens respond, "Lord, hear our prayer."

Close with the Our Father.

The Story of Thomas

Scripture: Jn 20:19-31
Feast: Second Sunday of Easter (A)
**Suggested Music: *Dream Journey* or "When You Seek
    Me"/*Gentle Sounds***

If Jesus walked into this room right this minute, would you believe he was Jesus? What would it take to prove to you that he was really Jesus? If you touched him, would you be able to tell that he was Jesus?

When Jesus was on earth people would often reach out to touch Jesus—it was a touch that they would always remember. It was a touch so filled with love they could feel it flow through their bodies. It was a touch that would last a lifetime.

We cannot reach out and touch Jesus with our hands today but we can always feel the closeness of him. Thomas, one of Jesus' faithful followers, had a hard time believing. Using our imaginations let's relive this special moment. It is Easter Sunday evening. You are one of Jesus' disciples. Will one touch be enough for you to believe?

Meditation

Close your eyes....Stretch out your arms....Let them go limp, falling to a comfortable position....Relax....Take a deep breath....Let it out slowly....Whisper, "Jesus."....

One by one, you have crept into an old building standing on the edge of the city....Slowly you ease yourself up the old wooden stairway so that no one will hear you....Creak! groans the step....A chill goes through you....Shhh!....You feel your

heart pounding against your chest....Roman soldiers cover the
streets like the web of a spider....You never know where they
will be until it's too late....They are hunting for friends of
Jesus, searching every nook and cranny of every building and
every dark street....

You are now inside the darkened room. Peter moves over to
the door, pulling the lock shut....James closes the window
shutters, shutting out the last glimmer of light....You are afraid
to light a candle....The room is crowded and warm....People
speak in whispers....You hear a woman sobbing....A voice
from the darkness speaks...."The tomb was empty!"....

You huddle in the darkness, feeling all alone....Suddenly, Jesus
is standing in front of you...."Peace, my friend," Jesus
whispers....Jesus knows that you are frightened....He reaches
out to comfort you....He turns his hands palms up....Wounds
create empty craters in his wrists....His side lies open like a
slab of meat....Jesus looks directly at you now, the light from
the candle flickering across his face...."Do you believe?" he
asks. (*Pause for a moment.*) Thomas is absent and has not
seen the risen Lord....

Later the same evening, you walk with a few disciples to
Thomas's home, crouching in the shadows....The disciples tell
Thomas what they have seen....Thomas stands shaking his
head....He does not believe....You tell Thomas about the
wounds in Jesus' hands, the wound in his side....Thomas turns
his back and walks away from you...."I'll believe when I can
touch the hands of Jesus myself....and put my hand into the
gash in his side."....You try one more time to make Thomas
believe....He leaves shaking his head in disbelief....

One week has past....You are once again locked in the small
room....Thomas sits close by your side in the darkness....
Clatter! Crash!....Listen to the footsteps of the Roman soldiers
in the street below....Fear tickles your spine....Grab for
Thomas' hand....The candle flickers....Voices are stilled....
Hear the quiet....Someone is standing beside you....It is
Jesus!...."Peace, my friends. Do not be afraid," Jesus

commands....You feel safer now....Nothing can harm you; no enemy can destroy you. Jesus stands beside you....

Jesus turns to your friend Thomas, "Touch the marks on my hands and feel the wound in my side."....Thomas slowly reaches forward, barely touching the hands of Jesus...."My Lord, my God," Thomas says, falling to his knees...."Thomas, you believed because you saw, but blessed are people who believe but have not seen me."

You feel like laughing, shouting....Happiness lights the room....You will always remember this moment....Jesus takes your hand into his and holds it tightly for a moment....Can you feel his touch?....Feel his warm hand grasp yours....You feel love....You feel truth....

Jesus looks within your eyes, asking, "Do you believe, my friend?" I will leave you alone with Jesus to answer his question.

Prayer
Jesus, I want to believe in you. I need to believe in you to provide the strength in my life. I do believe in you. May your Holy Spirit help me to grow in faith and in love. Amen.

Jesus is once again surrounded by his friends....Reaching out across the crowd, he places a hand on your shoulder....Turn and walk down the narrow stairway and out into the streets below....Open your eyes and return to this room.

Discussion

- Is it difficult for you to believe in things that you have not seen or experienced?

- If someone you really trust tells you something, will you believe it?

- Complete this sentence, "If I were Thomas and this happened to me, I would feel...."

- How can you feel the presence of Jesus in your world?

Dwell within My Love

Scripture: Jn 15:1-17
Feast: Fifth Sunday of Easter (B)
Suggested Music: *Dream Journey* **or "When You Seek Me"/**
Gentle Sounds

I am going to a workshop based on the elements of geophysics. Would you like to go with me? Most of us could not understand a talk on geophysics, or on Einstein's theory of relativity; we probably would not be interested in hearing the talk let alone understanding it.

People thronged to hear Jesus speak because he talked about situations that they could understand and incorporate into their own lives. Many of his followers were shepherds or worked in vineyards, and some were farmers. His followers could relate to the stories. Jesus was very careful to make sure the people could grasp what he was saying. If Jesus were alive today, what topics would he choose to talk about?

"I am the vine, and you the branches. He who dwells in me, as I dwell in him, will produce much fruit; for apart from me you can do nothing" (Jn 15:5). What does this mean to you? Would you be able to have more understanding if you had worked in a vineyard?

Why don't we relive those days and see if Jesus speaks to our hearts as well. Listen carefully to the words of Jesus.

Meditation

Stretch out....Make yourself comfortable....Close your eyes....
Shrug your shoulders....Relax....Take a deep breath....Let it
out slowly....Whisper, "Jesus."....

You enter a small crowded room....It is Passover....Jesus sits
on the floor with his disciples. Pillows soften the rough
wooden planks....The table is cluttered with cups and bowls....
Food remains on the serving platters....A half-eaten loaf of
bread and a goblet of wine is sitting on the table in front of
Jesus; a red drop of wine falls from the edge of the goblet,
staining the table linens....The red stain seeps into the cloth....
Paul the disciple leans forward, beckoning for you to join them
around the table....Jesus looks up and smiles as you take your
place beside Philip....Philip is not much older than you, his
young smooth skin a contrast to that of Peter....Whispering in
your ear, he tells you, "We have just shared the bread and
wine. Jesus says that he is going to be leaving us, but we don't
know why."....Jesus begins to speak...."I will not abandon you
like ships at sea. There is not much time left before I will be
gone from this world."....The disciples murmur, talking among
themselves....Jesus strikes the side of a cup to get your
attention...."I have much to say; allow me the time to
speak."....Jesus, glancing your way, asks, "My friend, if you
were the branch of the vine that produced these grapes, and
the gardener approached with a knife to cut you free of the
vine, would you be pleased?"....Words stick in your mouth....
Shake your head, thinking about the results of this action....
Jesus reaches over the table, placing his hand on your head, "I
am the real vine, and my Father is the gardener. Every barren
branch of mine he cuts away; every fruiting branch he cleans
in order that they have larger crops. God has already tended
you by pruning you back for greater strength and
usefulness."....

You wonder what this has to do with you, but you remain
silent....Paul rests his head in his hands, deep in thought....
Jesus rises from the table....He walks the length of the room.
"Dwell in me, as I in you. No branch can bear fruit by itself,

but only if it remains united with the vine."....You feel puzzled by this....Jesus, noticing your expression turns his attention directly to you....He walks as though a burden is upon his shoulders....He kneels on one knee by your side....The disciples are busy talking among themselves....Jesus takes this break to speak to you alone...."Friend, do you understand that apart from me you can do nothing?"...."Are there things in your life that need pruning? Is there time for me in your world?" (*Pause.*)

I will leave you alone with Jesus for a few minutes. Open your mind and heart to him.

Prayer

My Lord, my God, fill me with your Spirit. Open my eyes to your truth. Open my heart, allowing the fruit of your love to ripen within me. Thank you, Lord. Amen.

The visit has come to an end. Tell Jesus goodbye for now. Rise and walk through the doorway and down the rocky pathway. Open your eyes and return to this room.

Discussion

In small groups discuss the following:

• What was Jesus' command to us?

• If you were one of the disciples, what would you learn from this parable?

• What does this story mean in your own life?

• If God appeared before you as the gardener, what would he do with you?

• On those days that you feel cut off from the "vine" and everything is going wrong, what do you do to get in touch again?

Closing

In their small groups, ask the teens to spend a few minutes in prayer. Each one is asked to say a short prayer—a word of thanks or a request for help about something or someone in his/her life. Form a large group when completed. Join hands and pray the Our Father.

Jesus Makes a Promise

Scripture: Jn 14:23-29
Feast: Sixth Sunday of Easter (C)
Suggested Music: *Dream Journey* or "I Will Never Forget You"/*Gentle Sounds*

I am going to begin by asking you a few questions. Do you always find it easy to love every single person in your life? How about the guy who hangs out behind McDonald's, waiting for the last load for the dumpster? Is it easier to laugh at the poor guy's plight or to feel sadness over his situation? Hard questions to be sure—you are not unusual if you find it difficult to love everyone who may reside in your home, let alone feel a strong bond of love for the man by the dumpster. If we find these actions difficult, then we must realize that the heart of Jesus' message is to love all people, even those who are not lovable.

Jesus knew that loving others would at times be very difficult for us so he promised to send us a Paraclete. What is a paraclete? A paraclete is someone who stands beside us when we have a difficult action to take, giving us courage and support. The Paraclete in this case was the Holy Spirit.

Can anyone describe the action of the Holy Spirit? The Holy Spirit nudges us to do good things. Maybe this example will help. Can you see the wind? We can see what the wind picks up and moves from place to place, but the wind is invisible. Then how do we know it is there? We feel it in different ways. We cannot see the Holy Spirit, but the Spirit of Jesus is in us and is there to strengthen and guide us in our time of doubt and fears. The Holy Spirit is with us through our baptism. The

111

Spirit can fill us with joy and happiness. The Spirit is like the breath of God.

Jesus made a promise to his followers that the Holy Spirit would always be with us. After Jesus' death, the apostles were living in fear that Jesus' enemies would find them also. They felt as though Jesus had abandoned them even though Jesus appeared once before to some of his disciples. When Jesus did appear to them once again, he wanted to set their minds at rest and he greeted them with "Peace be with you!" Let's release our imaginations and experience the peace of Jesus.

Meditation

Close your eyes....Find a comfortable position....Let your arms fall loosely at your sides....Take a deep breath....Let it out slowly....Whisper, "Jesus."....Relax....

The evening finds us sitting in silence in the darkened upper room. Windows are boarded shut....The air is heavy and stale....One tiny candle lights the crowded room....It seems like a bad dream; everyone is caught in the shadows of the night....They speak in hushed voices....Peter, his head in his hands, sobs quietly, "My friend, my Lord, has abandoned me."....Place your hand on Peter's shoulder....Feel Peter's sadness....Remember how you felt when your best friend moved away or someone you really cared about died....Tears form in your eyes....Wipe your eyes....A shadow of a man is cast on the walls before you....Turn around....It is Jesus!....He places his hand above your head, "Do not be afraid, my friend. May my peace be with you."....The room brightens with the light of Christ....Your burdens become light....Your worries disappear and your tears turn to a soft smile....Jesus moves quickly now among the disciples, reassuring them that he will never leave them alone to face life's hardships....Peter collapses at Jesus' feet....Jesus takes Peter's rough, callused hands in his, helping Peter to his feet. "I love you, Peter," Jesus says gently....Turning his attention to the others, he speaks once again...."Where two or three are gathered in my name, I am with you. You will never be alone again. My Father is going to send the Holy Spirit, who will teach you everything and remind you of all that I have said."....

Jesus walks through the crowded room, stopping to reach out and touch those whose arms and hands reach toward him. A feeling of well-being and safety spreads through the room....At last, he walks back to where you are standing, your back touching a darkened corner of the room. Bending on one knee, he calls you by name. "Never be afraid, my dear friend. Let your heart be at peace. I promise you that you will never stand alone again. I will always be with you."....A feeling of warmth, the feeling of loving, and an awareness of the hardships of others fills your heart....Slowly he surrounds you with his strong arms and whispers, "Recognize these feelings of love for others; let them take root in your heart."....Holding you close he adds, "I love you."....Bask in his warmth for a moment. (*Pause briefly.*) Jesus continues, "I know that it is not always easy to love your enemies. It is not always easy to love members of your family." Jesus softly strokes your back, then questions, "Do you allow your friends to make it difficult for you to be a loving person? Is it at times easier to only think of your own needs for comfort?"....Quiet and peace surround you. I will give you a few minutes to talk to Jesus. Speak to him with your heart....

Prayer

Jesus, at times I grow callous and hardened to your "nudge," a reminder to offer your love and peace to others. I spend time worrying about what my friends will think of me and not enough time with you. For all the times it is difficult for me to act in loving ways, fill me with your Spirit, Jesus. May I live in your peace forever. Amen.

The light of dawn calls an end to the shadows of night. It is now time for you to make your way quietly down the back stairway....Glance back once more, then walk out into the early morning air....Open your eyes and return to this room.

Discussion

- Is there anyone who would like to share a time in your life when you felt the presence of the Holy Spirit? Or perhaps a time when fear overwhelmed you, only to be replaced with the strength you needed.

- What are some ways that we can show others the "peace of Christ"?

Prayer Service

Supplies: Bible opened to Jn 14:23-29, large candle, background music or "Come Holy Spirit"/In the Spirit We Belong.

Lower the lights. Ask the young people to take a few minutes in silence to think about the one person in their life whom they find it difficult to love. Have them ask the Holy Spirit to help them love even the unlovable.

Invite the teens to form a circle around the lighted candle. Read from the Bible, first raising it above your head reverently then returning it to a place of honor.

Leader: May the world become a more peaceful place where people learn to forgive. May the world be filled with the joy of the Lord. May we extend the love of Christ to those we find unlovable. Open our eyes and our hearts to the peace of our Lord.

Offer a sign of peace to the person next to you. Now, invite the students to offer the sign of peace to each other, saying, "May the peace of our Lord be with you always."

Close with praying the Our Father.

Pentecost

Scripture: Jn 20:19-23
Feast: Pentecost (ABC)
Suggested Music: *Dreamland* or "Only a Shadow"/*Gentle Sounds*

Though we are aware of the wind's actions when gusts of a fall wind send golden leaves scurrying across the yard, we are unable to see the wind. The soft gentle breeze of an electric fan on a summer evening can only be felt or experienced. The Holy Spirit is much like the movement of air: to only be experienced, not seen. The Holy Spirit gives us courage and strength to do what is right. It is the feeling of peace within our grasp. Jesus has promised us the gift of the Spirit to enable us to continue his work, giving us strength to walk with our Lord.

After Jesus' death, his friends were very frightened, going and coming only in the dark of night, sneaking through the shadows to reach the stairway to the upper room. They gathered together waiting and hoping Jesus would once again appear. Let's release our imaginations to join his followers in the upper room and experience the coming of the Holy Spirit.

Darken the room, lighting one candle. Ask a helper to stand among the students, greeting them with "Peace be with you!"

Meditation

Close your eyes....Find a comfortable position....Tense your body for fifteen seconds, then relax your head and neck, then your back, let your arms go limp, then relax your legs and feet....Take a deep breath....Let it out slowly....

It is nightfall....Darkness begins to cover the day with shadows....You are moving through the darkened streets, looking first to the right and then to the left....No one is following you....You slowly make your way up the creaking stairway....At last, Peter opens the small door to the room....

Candles flicker.... Shadows dance across the crowded room, bouncing off the frightened faces....The door creaks and whines behind you....Three more people come into the room....The air is heavy and stale....The windows are boarded shut....People speak in soft whispers, hoping the night air will not carry the sound of their voices to the street far below.

You recognize Mary, the mother of Jesus. She sits quietly by the door....A tear falls from her cheek....John stands closely by, his hand on her shoulder....Walk over to Mary....Wrap your arms about her shoulders....Take a moment to speak to Mary. (*Pause.*)

A knock on the door shatters the quiet....Move to a darkened corner of the room....Peter opens the door....James the apostle makes his way into the room...."The Roman soldiers are searching the houses for us....We need to be very careful on this night," James says in a loud whisper....Peter moves to the light of a candle, his rough red beard framing his face. "If only Jesus were here."....The words of Peter hang in mid-air....Without warning, the sound of surging wind fills the room, reminding you of the whistling sound of wind whipping through treetops....The whole house shakes beneath your feet....Doors rattle....Boards on the windows break, setting the hurricane winds free....The candles and lanterns flicker, then die away....You feel the gust rushing through your hair....Before you can move or speak, a subdued light covers the room....You can see light in the shape of flames above everyone's head....Looking up, you see the tongues of fire above your own head....

No longer do you feel fear....A calm settles over everyone in the room....Peace covers you like a warm blanket on a cold winter's night....Feelings of happiness and joy start at your toes and flow into your heart....This is like the happiness of Christmas morning and birthday surprises....Let the feeling of joy and the lightness of life fill your being....Enjoy the moment....

"It is the Holy Spirit!" Peter shouts...."Jesus kept his promise!" John adds excitedly. People move about the room joyfully laughing, dancing....Peter takes your hands and leads you to the center of the room...."Be happy, my friend. The Spirit of the Lord is truly with you!" he shouts....You feel the warm breath of God rush through you....

The windows and doors stand open now....Everyone is rushing to the streets below....You look out the window....A crowd has gathered....Leave the window; rush down the stairs into the starlit night....There is dancing in the street....You begin to feel the strength and courage to tell others of the love you feel for Jesus, for your family and friends....The Holy Spirit will help you to show love to others even when it is most difficult. Take a moment to feel the happiness....to feel the freedom.... There is no need to worry about what others will think of you for within your heart there is the peace of the Lord....

Take a moment to ask the Holy Spirit to guide you in your life choices....to experience the love of God for yourself....and the ability to show love to the lovable and the unlovable. (*Pause.*)

It is time to leave now....Wave goodbye to those gathered in the square....Remember, the Holy Spirit is within you when you love, when you share happiness and peace....Make your way down the cobblestone street....Open your eyes and return to this room.

Discussion

Form small groups and share the answers, one at a time, to the following questions:

- Share a time in your life when the Holy Spirit has made himself especially known to you.

- How do you deal with feelings of doubt and failure? Or do you?

- If you could ask one question of Jesus about your own faith life, it would be ....

Prayer Time

Supplies: bowl(s) of clear warm water, several hand towels

Ask the teens to come forward for a blessing. You and one helper (depending on the size of your group) dip your hand in the water and sign the forehead, lips, and heart of each teen:

May the grace of the Holy Spirit open your mind to the word of God. (*Sign forehead.*)

May the grace of the Holy Spirit be upon your lips that you will speak with love, without gossip and condemnation. (*Sign lips.*)

May the grace of the Holy Spirit fill your heart and soul with the love of God. (*Sign heart.*)

Conclude with the following prayer:

Leader: Let us now pray for the peace of Jesus and the coming of the Holy Spirit.

Invite the teens to respond, "We are one in the Spirit. We are one in the Lord."

Leader: Let us pray that the world will become a more peaceful place. (*Response*)

Invite the young people to offer prayers of petition.

Leader: For these needs and all the needs of your children, we pray to you, O Lord. (*Response*)

Part III

Ordinary Time

A Time for Celebration, a Time for Service

Scripture: Jn 2:1-12
Feast: Second Sunday in Ordinary Time (C)
Suggested Music: *Dream Journey*

Is there anything you've ever wanted to do but weren't old enough—drive a car, get a job, go away to school? Sometimes we want to do things, but the time is just not right. Did Jesus ever feel the same way? What happened at the wedding in Cana? The first time Jesus was asked to show he was sent from God, he probably wasn't sure whether or not he was ready, and he probably wasn't sure his followers were ready either. But he went ahead and helped his friends. He showed everyone—his friends, his disciples, his mother, the wedding guests—God's love.

Let's travel with our imaginations to a time that Jesus knew would begin his three years of ministry. Was Jesus really ready?

Meditation

Find a comfortable position....Close your eyes....Shrug your shoulders, releasing the muscles....Take a deep breath....Let it out slowly and whisper,"Jesus."....

The disciple James hands you an envelope....Break the wax seal....You have been invited to join Jesus and his friends at a wedding in Cana....Jesus packs a small knapsack for the journey....Glancing your way, Mary smiles. "Remember to pack something to eat on the way."....Everyone is in a happy mood....Jesus is carefree and laughing....

It is almost dark....The setting sun casts its shadows over the countryside....A cool breeze whisks across the desert land.... Listen, there is music in the distance....Mary calls out, "There it is! We made it! Knock on the door, my friend, and let them know that we are here."....Knock as hard as you can on the thick wooden door....Does anyone hear you?....The bridegroom answers the door....Smiling, he hugs Jesus and Mary, then welcomes everyone to his home....Wonderful tall cakes, sweet date cookies, and sugared fruits are being served....It reminds you of Christmastime at home....After several hours of party and music, Mary speaks quietly in Jesus' ear: "They do not have any more wine."....Jesus frowns, then questions, "Why are you telling me about this? It is not time for people to know who I am."....His answer surprises both you and Mary.

Mary walks over to the six large wine jars, tipping them on their side....A small dribble of wine forms a lacy pattern on the floor....There is very little wine and so many people....Mary beckons for you...."Child, go to those who are serving and tell them to do whatever Jesus tells them."....Work your way through the crowded room....Find the servants and send them to Jesus....Jesus looks startled, maybe a little annoyed. "Fill those jugs with water," he orders....The servers begin filling the jugs with water from the well....After the jugs are filled, Jesus instructs the servant to empty some of the water from the jugs into the pitcher you are holding...."Take the pitcher to the head waiter to taste," Jesus instructs....Be careful not to spill....The waiter did not see what happened, so when he tasted the water which Jesus had turned into wine he spoke to you, "This is the finest wine I have ever tasted! You have saved the best for last!"....and so the first miracle that Jesus worked was at Cana in Galilee.

The wedding guests partied until dawn....Then one by one they began the journey to their homes. At last you are alone with Jesus....He is tired but happy....Mary is very proud of her son....Jesus explains, "My mother, Mary, believed that I could do something about the problem of running out of wine....I wasn't ready to reveal God's glory and power....But, now I see that the time was right. With this sign I revealed God's glory." Jesus reaches out taking your hand in his and makes his way out into the garden....The sweet smell of honeysuckle hangs heavy in the night air...."Come and join me," he says as he gestures for you to take the seat next to his....Jesus settles back on the wooden swing near the sweetness of the rose garden....

The soft voice of Jesus breaks the silence of the evening air.... "If you could choose any miracle to help you or someone you know, what would you ask of me?"....Settle back against the seat, allow Jesus to know what is on your heart....

I will leave you alone with Jesus for a moment.

Prayer

Jesus, I too have felt unsure of what is being asked of me. Uncertain, I ask myself, "Is this the right time?" Help me to remember that just as the water was turned into wine, your love will change my life. Amen.

It is time for you to leave....Walk through the garden gate....Turn and wave goodbye....Open your eyes and return to this room.

Discussion

* Why did Mary believe Jesus could do something about the lack of wine? Do you think that she really understood?

* How do you think that Jesus must have felt?

* Why do you think that turning water into wine would be the first miracle when there were so many other important things to do?

* Do you need a miracle in your life right now?

Closing

Form a circle, holding hands. Pray a Hail Mary.

Invite prayer petitions and have the teens respond, "Lord, hear our prayer."

Turn On the Word — Listen to the Voice of God

Scripture: Mt 4:12-23; Mk 1:14-20
Feast: Third Sunday in Ordinary Time (AB)
Suggested Music: *The Sea* or "By Name I Have Called
    You"/*Gentle Sounds*

Supplies: radio or tape player, candle, music tape, list of student's names (optional)

Bring a radio. Begin by showing the radio.

How do you like the beat—would you prefer "rap" to this? You probably are wondering if I am hearing things. Let me make it easier for you. (*Turn on the radio.*) When I turn it on, we can all hear the music. If you knew you could win a prize by answering a phone quiz, how often would you listen? How often would you "study" so that you could win the prize?

In order to hear what is in this little piece of plastic we must first turn it on, and then we must listen. If we turn it off (*turn off radio*), we cannot hear the music or message.

God's word, the message, is always here just like the music but first we must turn it on by reading the word. Then we must tune in to God. God calls us by name but if we are not listening we will not be able to hear the call.

In Jesus' day, there were two types of rabbis. One taught Jewish boys to read and write, and the other was called a

Master Rabbi, a teacher's teacher. It was considered a great honor to be asked to study to be a rabbi. Families were expected to accept full responsibility for the man's family and expenses. Their families would have considered them foolish not to have accepted.

In those days, the world didn't have radios and TVs; Jesus needed help in getting his message across. Help came when four fishermen "tuned in to God" as they were casting their nets out to sea. When Jesus first spoke with the four fishermen about becoming his disciples or students, little did they understand the task ahead. The four fishermen thought Jesus' offer was like finding a golden egg beneath the goose. But if the four men had known what was really being asked of them, would they have answered so quickly? Let's release our imaginations to join the fishermen on the shore of the Sea of Galilee.

Meditation

Find a comfortable position....Close your eyes....Tense your body, then release your hands and arms....Feel the calm move over you....Take a deep breath....Whisper, "Jesus," as you let your breath out slowly....

You are walking on a sandy beach by the Sea of Galilee.... Time moves slowly as you wait for Jesus....The water slides in across the sand, leaving its wet fingerprints upon the ground....Gentle waves of sea water splash against your legs....The fragrance of sea grasses wafts in the summer breeze....The air is fresh and clear....Fishermen prepare their boats to go to sea, loading nets and bait on the rolling wooden decks....As you walk, wet sand curls around your toes....Step heavily into the sand; the next rolling wave erases the footprint, washing it out to sea....Fishermen are sitting by their boat, rolling a heavy net....They have long beards, strong shoulders, and hands rough with calluses.... You are able to hear them talking happily as they work.

Look out across the water....A small boat bobs like a cork in a bathtub sea of foaming bubbles....The fishermen wave....

Looking closer, you recognize one of the men....It is Jesus!....
Look closely....Jesus stands on the bow, his tattered jeans
rolled to his knees; his white T-shirt has seen better days....It is
your Jesus, today's Jesus....

The fishing boat rolls up on the shore....Sea water washes a
path in the wet sand....Jesus, looking weary, steps out of the
boat....Run down the shore to meet him....He is smiling as he
calls out your name....Listen; your name bounces off the
hillside and echoes across the waters....The echo calls you
over and over again....Approaching, Jesus smiles as he
reaches out to take your hand...."Thank you for coming to
meet me," Jesus says, giving you a casual pat on the
shoulder....Jesus gently takes your arm, leading you down the
rocky beach. The rushing sea waters chase your footsteps
across the sand....Water drips from the rolled legs of Jesus'
jeans...."Do you see those fishermen pulling in their nets?" he
asks...."I have come to see if those guys will take a chance and
help me out a little. There is a lot of stories to be told," he
says idly. He motions for you to wait on the shore for him....
Jesus takes long firm steps toward the docking boat....The
fishermen look up, barely seeming to notice him....Their
expressions change quickly when Jesus begins to speak to
them, calling them by name, just as he did you....Within a few
minutes they stop their labors and listen carefully....Placing
their folded nets in the boat, they join Jesus in returning to
where you stand waiting...."Meet my new friends." You take
the rough hand of Peter....His brother, Andrew, appears to be
much younger, his hands less scarred from life upon the sea....
Andrew's blue eyes twinkle with excitement....Join the small
group of men and continue walking along the shore....Jesus
stops abruptly, pointing toward a small boat preparing to leave
the shore....Two men are pushing the old boat out into the
water....Jesus walks more quickly now, calling, out, "Hey
guys! I've got a proposition for you. A whole new life waits for
you. James, John, come on back!"....The men look quizzically -
at Jesus, but almost automatically they return to shore....Are
they just curious, or do they know something that you
don't?....Jesus glances at you with a knowing smile....He

invites them to join the group....Putting away their lines and nets, they too make a decision to hang out with Jesus....

The small band of men begin a journey that will last a lifetime....Your feet are blistered; the sun lies hot upon the back of your head....The four chosen men walk happily along, chatting excitedly....James speaks out, "I really don't know why I came along. I just figured, 'Why not?'."....Day soon turns to night; shadows cross the valley....Jesus smiles at you, placing his hand on your shoulder. Feel the warmth of his hand....Leaving the others to prepare for their journey across the sea, you and Jesus walk to a small bonfire on the edge of the shore....Settle yourself in the sand....Jesus leans forward, warming his hands by the fire, then takes your hands in his.... He questions, "Will you stick with me? I'm going to be there for you, no matter what comes up."....The weight of the responsibility falls heavily upon your mind...."What do I give up? What can I do?.... What will my friends think?" and finally, "You must be kidding, Lord." You wonder how four men, some twice your age, could answer so quickly....Jesus leans forward on his haunches, "Do you have questions, my friend?" he asks knowingly....Take a few minutes to talk with Jesus. (Pause until students become restless.)

Prayer

Jesus, my Lord, open my ears to your call. Open my mind to your teaching. Open my heart to the warmth of your love. Steady my uncertain steps as I go down life's path. Amen.

Discussion

Leader: The moral qualities we will need on our journey are: humility, gentleness, and patience. As Christians we should always strive to help one another and attempt to preserve unity and peace in our homes and in our lives.

- Do you think that the four fishermen had as much knowledge as you have about Jesus, or more knowledge? Did this make their decision easier or were there other factors?

- What is being asked of you if you answer Jesus' call?

- What if you fail one day to live like a Christian follower?

Activity: "Chart Your Christian Journey"

The four fishermen were about to embark on a spiritual journey that would change the world forever. How has your spiritual journey changed your life?

Think about your first memories of Jesus, when you first spoke to him or thought about him. Then think through all the highs and lows of your relationship with him from your first encounter until now.

Ask each student to draw a line graph of his/her spiritual journey. Starting at the left side of page, which is the person's date of birth, draw a horizontal line. Movement upward indicates times when they grew closer to God, while movement downward shows periods when they felt cut off from Jesus. Instruct them to put an "X" in the peaks and valleys of the line to represent significant events in their spiritual lives.

The bottom of the page should indicate this time frame: "Birth," "Six Years Old," "Junior High," "Last Year," "Last Summer," and "Today."

Students should label things that have caused them to think about Jesus, times when Christian friends or family have helped them, or times when a retreat was meaningful.

You may want to chart your own journey to share with the class. Allow a short time for drawing the chart and then ask volunteers to talk about what their graph tells about them.

Closing Prayer

Spend a few moments in silent prayer to think about how closely you have walked with Jesus lately. If you fell off the path, how can you get back on track? Contemplate what you need to work out before you are ready to continue your journey with Jesus.

Let's close in silent prayer. As we pray, consider your relationship with Jesus. How have you responded to his love?

Allow time for silent meditations. Form a circle, holding hands as a community. Ask for prayer petitions then conclude with the Our Father.

Standing Up for What Is Right

Scripture: Lk 4:21-30
Feast: Fourth Sunday in Ordinary Time (C)
Suggested Music: *Bamboo Waterfall* **or "Pardon your
    People"/*Gentle Sounds***

Most of us have experienced at least one major move during
our lifetime. If you left your old neighborhood when you were
ten or eleven and went back to visit when you were sixteen or
seventeen, it is pretty safe to assume there were a lot of
changes in your life as well as in the lives of your friends. How
many of you have ever moved from one state to another, or
one town to another, or even across town? Did you go back to
visit? Was everything just like you left it? Probably not.
Nothing ever stays the same. Isn't it both sad and interesting
that home or our hometown is not always where we are
accepted and appreciated the most? Did Jesus have this problem?

Would the people from Jesus' old neighborhood welcome
Jesus with open arms? The answer to this may surprise you.
Jesus was hailed by the people in other villages but this would
not be the case in Nazareth. Jesus experienced the harshest
form of rejection by the people who should have known him
best. Let's release our imaginations to be with Jesus when he
returns to his boyhood home.

Meditation

Find a comfortable position....Close your eyes....Roll your
shoulders, allowing your arms to feel the heaviness of

slumber....Take a deep breath....Let it out slowly....Relax....
Look into the mirror of your life....Look at your own reflection....

You find yourself seated on a hard wooden bench within the
walls of a synagogue in a little town called Nazareth....The
people chatter among themselves, "I remember this kid when
he followed Joseph around doing odd jobs."...."Can you
imagine that some think he is the Messiah?" rings out
another....But there are those who feel pride that someone so
well thought of came from "their" town....Jesus places his
hand on your shoulder to steady himself as he slowly rises to
take his place of honor....Jesus begins to read from the scroll
of the prophet Isaiah, "The Spirit of the Lord is on me,
because he has anointed me to preach good news to the poor.
He has sent me to proclaim the year of the Lord's favor."....
Jesus rolls the scroll and hands it to you....Jesus continues
speaking, "This Scripture came true today!"....Jesus has
announced that he has been sent by God, that he is the
Messiah....The crowd moves forward, muttering to
themselves, "This cannot be. He is only Joseph's son." "You
speak in riddles!" shouts another....Jesus moves to take his
place once again....Jesus interrupts the crowd, "Listen when I
tell you that people never believe nor accept a prophet who
comes from their own town."....Boos and catcalls fill the
synagogue....Jesus continues, "When Elisha was a prophet,
there were many people in Israel who had leprosy. Why is it
then that the only leper who was healed by Elisha was
Naaman, a man who lived in Syria?"....The men come to their
feet, their voices raised. "God would not waste his powers on
this simple man," barks a man from the back of the room....
The awestruck crowd has quickly grown restless and angry....

Jesus sees the look of alarm on your face....He lays his
reassuring hand on your head...."Show us a miracle!"...."We
came for miracles!"...."Who are you kidding?" demands
another...."You are not sent by God. We knew you as a
boy."....Without warning, the people stand, raising their fists
in anger and disbelief....Old and young alike push forward,
grabbing Jesus and tossing him out the door of the

synagogue....A large, burly man throws Jesus to the ground....
In the shadows of darkness, you hide beneath the branches of
an olive tree. The people mob Jesus, taking him to the edge
of a hill to push him over the cliff...."Run, Jesus, run," you
whisper to yourself....Standing on the crumbling outcropping
of rock, Jesus calmly turns to study the crowd. Shaking his
head, he walks through their midst as though they did not
exist....Jesus calls his disciples to follow....Spotting your
shadow beneath the olive branches, he calls out, "Hurry, my
friend!"....Jesus vanishes into the night, away from those who
wish to kill him....Jesus stops now on the moonlit road,
waiting for you to catch up with him....

On the road to Capernaum he slows his pace, knowing that
you are very tired...."Jesus, you could have told the people
what they wanted to hear. You could have performed a
miracle or two....Why didn't you?....You could have saved all
this hassle."....Jesus studies the question for a few moments
then answers. "It was time to set a few things straight. I expect
the same of you....You could have done something, too....I
only heard your silence and the sound of running feet."....You
squirm uncomfortably....Your unspoken words drag on into
the silence of night....Jesus sees your discomfort and places
his arm around your shoulders, "I know that it is not always
easy to be laughed at when you speak up for what you believe
in, but this is what I ask you to do"....Jesus hesitates. "You
can do it, can't you?" (*Pause briefly.*)

Jesus stops to rest near the gates of the city of Capernaum....
Handing you the flask of water, he studies you closely....It is as
though he can see through you. He then speaks, "Close your
eyes for a minute and ask yourself this question. Is the
acceptance of your friends more important to you than the
acceptance of God?"....I will give you a few minutes to answer
Jesus. (*Pause.*)

Prayer
*Lord, it is hard to speak up for the right person or the
right idea. My friends may laugh. My family may not*

understand. Help me to deal with the feelings of rejection, the feelings of not being good enough. Give me the courage to stand by you regardless of the consequences. I ask this in your name. Amen.

Discussion

If you have a large group you may prefer breaking down into clusters of four to six students. Ask the groups to share answers to the following questions.

- Do you think that people always want to hear the truth?

- Why do you think the people of Jesus' hometown did not accept him?

- How do you deal with rejection? Can you accept it as a way of looking at your life and making corrections, or do you become angry or hurt?

- What forms of rejection do most of us face in our lifetimes?

Prayer Time: Prayers of Petition

Ask the young people to think of people in their lives whom they have failed to appreciate and encourage the way they should. Tell them to give thanks to God for placing these people in their lives.

Leader: Build us up, Lord. Let us feel the strength of the Holy Spirit. Bind us together as a community with your love. We offer these prayers of need and prayers of blessings. Lord, hear our prayer.

Invite students to mention the person or situation they wish for God to bless. Then have them respond, "Lord, hear our prayer."

The Beatitudes

Scripture: Mt 5:1-12
Feast: Fourth Sunday in Ordinary Time (A)
Sixth Sunday in Ordinary Time (C)
Suggested Music: *Dream Journey* or "Peace Is Flowing Like a River"/*Gentle Sounds*

Have you ever compared your life to that of a friend or a person you admire greatly? How did you come out—on top or on the bottom? Sometimes we set our sights too high. We make the path to success/happiness too difficult. Jesus explains that true happiness comes from God no matter what sadness we might be going through. He also tells us that we can't find all of our happiness in having fun, going to parties, or "living it up."

Following the birth of our second daughter, I told my father that I never knew happiness could be so complete. He smiled, patted me on the hand, and offered this advice, "Hold on to it. In the course of life it will only last a little while." Advice or pessimism? But over the years, when engulfed in reality I remember his words. How precious the times of happiness become.

Ask the young people to make a list of necessities for finding happiness. Complete the list with suggestions and then put it away for later.

What do you think Jesus means by "real happiness?" (*Encourage discussion*.) One day a crowd of people ask Jesus the same question. Let's release our imaginations, joining the crowd that surrounds Jesus.

Meditation

Find a comfortable position....Close your eyes....Allow your arms to fall limp into your lap....Take a deep breath....Let it out slowly....Whisper, "Jesus."....Relax....Look into the mirror of your life....Look at yourself....

It is early morning....The sun has just peeked over the top of the mountain....Your body feels cold and stiff....You fold your arms tightly across your chest, gathering your blanket about you....Last night your bed was the cold, hard ground....You have waited all night at the foot of the mountain where Jesus went to pray....You can hear the murmuring and shuffling of restless feet around you....Many people have gathered during the night, hoping to see and hear Jesus....Some have come expecting miracles....

The clouds slowly float into nothingness, no longer blocking the warmth of the sun....Lying on your back, you stretch your arms and legs like a lazy cat in the sunshine of your garden.... Today will be a good day....The crowd shifts its mass up the steep hillside....Their voices fill the day with loud excitement....Shouts of "Jesus is coming!" rise above the din of murmuring voices....The crowd quickly surrounds Jesus, reaching, pleading, clamoring to touch him....It has been said that to touch Jesus is to be healed....You observe many miracles on this day....Blind men dance in joy, their sight restored....A small, pathetic child rises from her deathbed to run and play among the children....Those who believe are healed....The curious are convinced the reign of God is at hand....

Jesus now moves back up the hill, above the crowd, so that everyone can see him....He appears almost as a small speck on the hillside....Strain to catch sight of him....Can you see him standing there surrounded by children? (*Pause.*) The wind blows Jesus' long dark hair....He reaches out to pull his hair from his face, fastening it back with a small leather thong.... Jesus glances about him....He is a happy man.... Feeling content you decide that this indeed is a good day!....

A young man, a year or two older than you, steps through the crowd surrounding Jesus and says, "Talk to me. How are we supposed to find happiness in this screwed-up world?".... Jesus, standing tall on the hillside, responds: "You are going to find happiness when you recognize that you are spiritually poor. Are you ready to admit that you don't know everything? (*Pause.*) Are you ready to admit that you need God and a few other people? (*Pause.*) You must admit your weakness and accept the help and love others give....All the money your pockets can hold won't buy this gift."....The crowd "oohs" and "aahs," nodding their heads in understanding....You shake your head in confusion....This doesn't sound anything like what you've heard before....Rise from your place on the barren knoll....Suddenly, it becomes important to be closer to Jesus....Make your way through the tangle of bodies and nervous feet....Jesus notices you working your way through the throng of people....Jesus motions for you to come and sit at his side....Take a seat on the dew-covered grass....He places a finger over his lips....It is time to be quiet and listen....

Jesus adjusts his belt and then begins to speak again, "You will be a happy person if you are able to show your feelings and allow others to share their pain with you." Looking down into your eyes he quietly asks, "Are you able to show others how you truly feel? (*Pause.*) Are you able to listen with your heart to the pain of others? (*Pause.*) If a tear were to creep down your cheek would you try to hide it or be honest about the pain you experience?"....A lump forms in your throat....Take time to answer Jesus. (*Pause.*)

Jesus continues, "Happy are those who show mercy to others. Be a light in their lives; brighten their days with your presence. Always try to make the world a better place." The crowd murmurs in approval....Jesus walks back and forth across the width of the hillside....Coming back to where you are resting, your back against the harshness of the rock, he asks you, "Are you able to give of yourself to others without thought of what you may receive in return? (*Pause.*) Can you be this way with your brother or sister? (*Pause.*) Is it easier to show your good side to a friend than to your own family? A gift with no strings attached is truly a Godly gift." I will give you time to answer Jesus. (*Pause.*)

"Happy are those whose greatest desire is to do what God requires. God should be 'number one' in your life."....A rousing cheer fills the air....Sitting on the outcropping of rock, Jesus takes time to question you once again, "Do you know the difference between God's will and your will? (*Pause.*) There are many tough choices that you must make in your life. Do you really try to put God first?" (*Pause.*)

The sun begins to shield itself from the day....Shadows creep across the landscape....Jesus sips water from a flask. Wiping water from his lips, he continues, "Happy will be those who work for peace among men. Do you bring harmony or do you bring strife when you go through your front door?"....Jesus places his arm around your shoulders and whispers, "Peace begins in your heart and in your own home." Answer Jesus with your heart. (*Pause.*)

"You will be a happy person if you can stand up for what you believe in. People will respect you in the long run.".... Jesus walks to a patch of blooming wild flowers. Stooping over, he picks a bloom. Holding it to his nose, he breaths in the sweet fragrance, then continues, "It's rough to be called names and hated because of what you are. You know that I understand this, but you will find happiness if you can just turn them off. Shrug it off; just tell them, 'Whatever.' The only thing that really counts is what's going on between you and God.".... With gentleness hanging on every word he leans forward, asking, "My friend, are you the same person in school that you are in church? Do you make an effort to let God show through you?"....Answer your Lord....

At long last, the crowd sits in expectant wonder as Jesus continues...."Happy are the meek. Find a quiet spot within yourself. Listen to what God and others are trying to say. Walk in humility. Accept who you are and where you come from." Jesus raises his hands high above his head in a sign of peace...."If you do these things you shall truly be a child of God, and you will find all the happiness that your heart can hold." Jesus slowly turns from the people, signaling a time to close....Bending low on one knee, he places his hands on your head....You can feel the touch of his hands....He looks deep within your being and says, "You are a child of God....I love you." I will leave you with Jesus for a moment....Speak to him with your heart.

Prayer

Jesus, although at times I stand in the shadows of life, I do love you. Help me to always remember that true happiness in my life will come from knowing you. May I follow in your footsteps, reaching out to those needing your touch. Amen.

It is time for Jesus to continue his journey....Tell him goodbye for now....Make your way down the rocky hillside....Open your eyes and return to this room.

Discussion

Bring out the list you made earlier and ask the students:

- How do Jesus' instructions on finding happiness compare with our list? How are they different? How are they the same?

- What did Jesus mean, "Peace begins in your heart and in your own home?" How can we see that this happens.

- Jesus wants us to trust in God in times of sadness and difficulty. He tells us that if we trust in him, nothing can take our happiness away from us. How can we show that we trust God?

Prayer Time

Ask the students to give thought to the area of their own life where they feel they need the most support and to pray

27. The Beatitudes

for those who have been constant examples of God's love to them. Offer prayers in petition form.

Leader: Happy are we who give thanks to the Lord.

Invite the teens to respond, "Thanks be to God."

Leader: Happy are those who place their needs before God in prayer. (*Response*)

Leader: Happy are those who work for peace among all people. (*Response*)

Join hands in a circle. Pray the Our Father.

Salt and Light

Scripture: Mt 5:13-16
Feast: Fifth Sunday in Ordinary Time (A)
Suggested Music: *Dreamland*

You have the whole house to yourself. It is early evening, you put a movie on the VCR, and all is well. Not for long. The power goes out. Is it just your house, or is the whole neighborhood out?

In this situation, are you more apt to sit there and grumble, take a peek outside, or go get a candle and make the best of things? (*Invite discussion.*)

Whether you decide to do something about the problem or to be part of the problem is up to you. But I am not just talking about getting a candle out and lighting it.

Invite the teens to brainstorm, making a list of issues or concerns that demand attention, e.g., AIDS, teen pregnancy, child abuse, homelessness, pornography, abortion, etc.

What are you willing to do or are you willing to do anything about each one of these causes? Do you take the attitude, "Let somebody else to do it and I'll support it" or "What can *I* do? I am only one person"?

Everyday, situations exist and causes are born. Some we will believe in; others won't matter to us. However, in that decision-making process of deciding if you can make a difference, we touch upon issues of importance to Jesus.

Jesus was a great teacher because he always got his audience's attention. Jesus spoke about being the salt and light of the world. Let's release our imaginations, joining Jesus as he speaks about making a difference.

Meditation

Find a comfortable position....Close your eyes.... Relax....Your arms and legs are heavy....Take a deep breath....Let it out slowly....

It is early evening....The sun lies below the rooftops.... Flickering lights begin to appear in the windows, lighting the night....Jesus sits with his disciples, warming themselves by the heat of a sparking campfire....Jesus looks up and notices that you have joined them....Standing, he reaches out and takes your hand....He is glad that you have come...."Sit here, my friend," he says, touching the old fallen tree that has become a bench...."We're talking about making a difference in the world.

"I want to explain it this way," he continues....Looking directly at you, he speaks again. "You are the salt of the earth. If you were to use salt over and over again, eventually it would lose its flavor. If salt loses its flavor, you throw it upon the ground. It is of no further use."...."But, I don't cook that much," you interrupt....Jesus laughs out loud, not making fun of you, but understanding your confusion...."Let me do a better job explaining so that you will understand."....The disciples listen intently as Jesus explains, "We don't have a way to keep our food cool in summer. Salt preserves our meat. It then in turn seasons our food, making it more palatable. I told you that you were the 'salt of the earth,' meaning that you are capable of changing life's hardships. You can make a difference, making a better world to live in. But you have a free will and can make the decision to put blinders on and 'do your own thing.' I want you to realize that you have the ability to 'flavor' life, to make living easier for others."....The disciples murmur among themselves....Peter stands and stretches, then pulls a blanket around his shoulders, shielding him from the cool night air....

Jesus places a hand on your back, rubbing back and forth across your shoulders…."The earth has its problems; it needs you, your salt, your energy. There is a movie theater in your town that admits young people to see pornography. Do you care or do you ask, 'Where do I get in line?' (*Pause.*) Black smoke fills the air daily from the factories. Waste is dumped into your rivers. Is there something you can do? (*Pause briefly.*) Your friends are using hard drugs, killing their minds and their bodies. Drugs are sold in your school. Do you keep silent? Do you join them? Do you try to help or overlook the problem? (*Pause.*) Someone you know will die from AIDS. Do you ridicule the sick and dying or do your find compassion and awareness? (*Pause.*) Are there conditions or causes that touch your life? These are hard questions. Look within yourself." (*Pause.*)

Keep your eyes closed….Become aware of a strong light in the room….The image of Jesus sits nearby….His hand is outstretched….In the center of his palm, a ball of white light radiates his love, his forgiveness, his healing….Evening shadows are lifted….The figure of Jesus disappears from view….Only light lingers, chasing shadows from your life….

You and the light of Jesus are all that remain in the room…. Breathe in the light of Christ….Breathe the light of Christ into your whole being….Exhale….The light spreads once again throughout the room….The radiance shines from within, enveloping your body and soul….

The words of Jesus echo in your mind: "You are like light for the whole world. A city built on a hill cannot be hidden. No one lights a lamp to put it under a bowl. Instead he puts it on the lampstand, where it gives light for everyone in the house. In the same way your light must shine before people, so that they will see the good things you do and give praise to your Father in heaven. I am part of you and you are part of me."

Be aware only of your heartbeat….Breathe in the light of Christ….Exhale his love….his healing….his forgiveness….

Closing Prayer

Give each teen a taper.

Come forward with your taper and light it from the community candle to be a symbol of the light of Christ.

Allow a few minutes for silent reflection in this atmosphere.

May the light of Christ travel with us to illuminate our journey of faith. May the Lord cleanse us of sin and share with us his knowledge, hope, and understanding. Let us go in peace and may the Lord remain with us always. Amen.

Close with the Apostles' Creed.

The Wind and the Water

Scripture: Mk 4:35-42
Feast: Twelfth Sunday in Ordinary Time (B)
Suggested Music: *The Sea* or **"Song over the Water"**/*Instruments of Peace* or **"When You Seek Me"**/*Gentle Sounds*

Once when I was a child, I experienced the effects of a tornado—wind with such voracity, such strength, such terror, that even the sound of wind is still disquieting to my spirit. When I was a teen I lived in Arizona, well known for its flash floods. One moment the sun would be shining and the next, without warning, the heavens opened and rain fell in such abundance that you could not see your hand before your eyes. Dry riverbeds filled to overflow; small frame houses dissolved into the roaring waters.

The desert lands that Jesus called home and the river he set sail upon, the Sea of Galilee, are well noted for instant storms. The water is surrounded by hills. The wind whips around the base of the hillsides, each pass picking up in speed. Small craft find themselves in danger quickly. On a day such as this, the apostles found themselves in a windstorm of gargantuan proportions. Let's release our imaginations and find out what happened when the apostles met their match in nature.

Meditation

Find a comfortable position....Close your eyes....Shrug your shoulders, releasing the tension....Relax your arms and legs....Take a deep breath....Let it out slowly....Whisper, "Jesus."....Relax

You are sitting on the sandy shore of the Sea of Galilee waiting for Jesus to return....Water pushes into land, then rushes back into the sea leaving damp fingerprints on the muddy shore....Several small boats prepare to cast off.... Fishing nets and fishing poles are piled high....Peter moves about the deck of his boat storing food for the journey....He removes his cap, allowing the soft winds to pull through his snarled red hair....He calls out, "Ready to go."....John jumps upon the rocking deck, then leans over the side, offering you his hand....

Jesus is the last one to board....He takes his seat quietly, then looks over at you and smiles....He lays his head back upon the bow of the boat....The winds of fall are crisp and cool....Your hair blows across your face....Feel the gentle rolling of waves against the bottom of the boat....Jesus is fast asleep, his head rolling from side to side with the rhythm of the waves....Take off your jacket and cover the sleeping Jesus against the chill of the day....Peter, always in charge, whispers loudly, "Don't wake Jesus! Keep it down!"....A hush falls over the boat....All is silent except for the pounding of the waves....

Within moments, clouds cover the sunlit sky....A sound of a low, roaring rumble echo against the hills....Darkness covers the sea....Andrew grabs the port lantern and attempts to spark the oil-soaked rag....Waves of water wash over the deck, drenching you and the apostles....Jesus appears to sleep on in blissful slumber....The winds whistle and whine, tossing the boat like a small rubber toy in a bathtub....Grasp the railing.... Another wave assaults the small boat, nearly turning it upside down....Cold sea water drips from your hair....Bone chilling cold rushes through your body....Peter, water dripping from his beard, holds tightly to the wheel....He looks worried.... John and James pull the rope on the sails....James, slight of build, falls, nearly going overboard....Are you afraid?....The apostles cling to the railing and to each other....The winds sound their alarm....Cover your ears....Peter calls out, "Wake Jesus!"....Jesus sleeps on....

Andrew, his hands shaking with fright, crawls to your side.... "Go up to the bow of the boat and wake Jesus."....Holding on to the railing you make your way over the seats, past James and John....Place your hand on Jesus....Wake him....Andrew cries, "We are going down!"....

Jesus sits bolt upright....The wind fans his hair about his face....He looks down at his feet, now covered with cold dark waters from the sea....He glances about the small craft, noting the sails are ripped and torn....He wipes the water from his eyes....Noticing you, he pats your hand in reassurance....Ask Jesus for help....Jesus stands with his legs braced, swaying from side to side....He slowly raises his hands over the battling sea and commands, "Peace! Be stilled!"....As suddenly as it began, the winds stop....The sea is calm and smooth....The clouds are lifted and rays of sun touch the sea....Jesus pulls you to his side, looks at his confused friends, and questions, "Why were you afraid? Don't you believe in me?"

Peter, rubbing the stubble on his chin whiskers, asks, "Who are you, Jesus, that even the wind and sea obey you?".... Andrew leans forward and whispers in your ear, "The people hereabouts believe that the sea is a dwelling place of devils and evil spirits. Surely, Jesus must be sent by God!"....Peter does not wait for an answer; shaking his head he looks out across the calm sea....

Jesus takes your hands in his. "There is no shame in feeling fear. 'No fear, no gain,' I always say. Just call me when loneliness or fear walk into your life. I will always be here for you. Do you trust me with your life? (*Pause briefly.*) Will you allow me to be a part of *everything* that you do? Shield nothing from me."....

I will leave you alone so that you may talk with Jesus. If you live with fear in your life, share this with Jesus.

Prayer
Jesus, thank you for calming all the storms in my life.
Thank you, Lord, for your loving protection.
Strengthen me with your wisdom and guidance. Amen.

The boat pulls gently into shore....It is time to leave....Step out of the boat....Turn and walk down the shoreline....Open your eyes and return to this room.

Discussion

- What was Jesus attempting to teach his disciples by seeming to ignore the storm?

- When Jesus was awakened, why was he angry?

- In this story and in your life, what weakens your faith (e.g., fear, doubt, loneliness, anger, etc.)?

Activity: A Walk in Faith

Supplies: blindfolds for half of the students

Select a partner. Take turns wearing the blindfold. Each one will have chance to guide his/her blindfolded partner on a brief walk. It will be the responsibility of the "guide" to insure confidence in his/her partner, warning him/her of pending danger or obstacles. *The object is not to see how many times your partner can fall down or get hurt.* Call time and change places.

When the walk is complete ask each student how he/she graded his/her partner.

- Did you feel safe?

- What scared you?

Closing

Heavenly Father, we thank you for bringing us together to explore our faith in you and our faith in each other.

Hold hands and pray the Our Father.

The Good Samaritan

Scripture: Lk 10:25-37
Feast: Fifteenth Sunday in Ordinary Time (C)
Suggested Music: "Pardon Your People"/*Gentle Sounds*

Take a few minutes and list the names of six people with whom you communicate the most. Be sure to include someone at church and someone in your home. List them in order of importance in your life.

Now I want you to look at that list. Choose which person you would contact at four in the morning if you had a very big problem—someone who would keep your problems a secret.

• Whom would you call if you were down in the dumps and needed cheering up?

• Whom would you call if you found yourself needing to make a very big decision and you really needed good, informed advice?

• Think of a problem you recently faced. To whom did you go?

• Would these same people feel comfortable coming to you for the same reasons you chose them? Why or why not?

• How would you define this statement: "Love your neighbor as yourself"?

Jesus wanted us to understand that we are neighbors to everyone in the world. He wanted us to always be willing to share God's love with others, regardless of where they come from or what color their skin is. One day Jesus told a story about what it means to be a good neighbor. Why don't we join Jesus in the shade of an apple tree and listen as he tells this story.

Meditation

Find a comfortable position....Close your eyes....Allow your body to relax....Take a deep breath....Let it out slowly....
Whisper, "Jesus."....

Smell the sweet fragrance of apple blossoms....Look at the tree....Pink petals slowly fall to the ground....A carpet of green grass covers the meadow....Mountains stand as sentries around the edge of the meadow....There is the soft laughter of children playing in the distance....There is Jesus!....He is leaning against the crooked trunk of a tree. He wears khaki shorts and a green shirt. His sandaled feet are the only clue to his biblical identity. Jesus smiles and calls out your name....
Greet your friend....Jesus offers you a hardy handshake.
Clearly he is happy to see you here....Take a seat beside Jesus as he begins his story.

Men push to the front row as Jesus begins to speak....Children stand behind the men, jumping on one foot and then the next to be able to catch sight of Jesus....Women, some carrying children upon their backs, some carrying vessels of water, find room wherever they can, always to the rear of the crowd.
Jesus waits until the people are settled, then says...."You have asked me to explain what it means to love your neighbor....
This little story may help you to understand."....He glances over to you, then begins, "Once upon a time there was a man going from Jerusalem to Jericho. Now the road was very dangerous for people to travel. Robbers often hid behind the big rock boulders that line the roadway. And no one ever traveled on this road alone. But the man didn't think about the danger and began his journey alone. The worst happened not far from Jerusalem. Robbers attacked the man, stole all his money, took his clothes, and beat him very badly. The robbers thought him dead when they had finished. He was truly down and out for the count.

"A priest was walking down the same road. He saw the poor man lying by the side of the road but just kept walking. The next person who came by was a Levite, a person who worked in the Temple. He saw the man on the ground but kept on moving, closing his ears to the injured man's cries for help. Later in the afternoon another man came by. This man was from Samaria." Now remember, the Jews did not like the Samaritans, and the feeling was more than mutual. "But this Samaritan saw the man lying on the ground and felt sorry for him. The Samaritan came up to the poor bleeding man. He put bandages on him and washed his wounds as best he could. Then the Samaritan lifted him on his horse and took him to the nearest inn where he put him to bed and took care of him. The next morning the Samaritan gave the innkeeper money to take care of the man. He also told the innkeeper, 'If it costs more than I have given you, I will pay the rest when I come back.'"....Jesus sips water from a small clay cup, then asks a question, "Now which of these three men was a good neighbor?"....Everyone listening to the story begins murmuring among themselves. "The one who was kind and took care of him." "The Samaritan showed God's love," calls another from the crowd....Jesus nods his head in agreement, "Yes, now you understand. Now go out and treat others the way you want to be treated."

Jesus takes your hand in his....He leans very close, speaking quietly, "I know that it is hard to be a good neighbor when everyone else isn't. I know the world teaches you to 'take care of number one.' That Samaritan was the only one to stop because he knew what it was like to be hurting and have people pass by. It's as simple as that."....Jesus stands; then, walking beneath the branches of the apple tree, he questions you...."When you see someone in trouble, is your first thought that someone else will take care of the problem, so you can look the other way? (Pause.) Can you turn around and walk away when someone keeps chipping away at you? (Pause.) Can you give your time and patience to a friend? Family? Stranger? (Pause briefly.) With whom do you have the hardest time?"....

I will leave you alone with Jesus. Take a few minutes to talk with him.

Prayer

Dear Jesus, at times I think that I am too busy to help others, leaving the problem for someone else to clean up. Open my eyes, my heart, and my ears to the needs of others. Steady my walk with you. Steady my walk with others, especially those who are ignored, forgotten, or whose skin color is different from mine. Thank you, Jesus, for the love you give. Amen.

It is time for you to leave....Take Jesus' hand....Remember his words as you walk away....Open your eyes and return to this room.

Discussion

- Can anyone share a time when you had an opportunity to act like a good neighbor and you blew it?

- Can anyone share a time when you were the good neighbor?

- Who would you say is your "good neighbor"?

Activity

Invite the students to act out the parable but with modern-day situations. If the group is large enough you may want several smaller groups to take part. Let them choose the scene and the dialogue. The moral must remain the same. Then ask each group to come forward and perform its skit for the others.

Optional Activities

- Invite the students to retell the story, bringing in as many details as possible.

- Have the teens sit together in a group. Pick a panel of six judges. Select students to act the role of the Levite, priest, and Samaritan. Ask the judges to call "witnesses" to the scene as well as the main participants. The "judges" will try to determine if anyone had a good excuse for not coming to the aid of the Samaritan. The "judges" can allow the audience to participate in questioning also.

Closing

Stack hands in the center of a circle. In the spirit of oneness with the Lord, pray the Our Father.

The Parable of the Buried Treasure

Scripture: Mt 13:44-52
Feast: Seventeenth Sunday in Ordinary Time (A)
Suggested Music: *Dream Journey* or "By Name I Have Called You"/*Gentle Sounds*

What would you do if one day while helping to clean up the backyard you found a buried treasure? Or perhaps that lottery ticket that your friend gave you actually was drawn? Think about this for a few minutes: What are the first four things that you would do with the found riches? (*Make a list on the board or newsprint from student's suggestions.*)

Would spending your "treasure" this way make you happy?

One evening in the early fall, Jesus spoke to his friends about this same question. However, surprisingly, Jesus didn't come right out and tell his friends what he thought they should do with this newfound treasure. Instead he told them a story. Let's release our imaginations and listen to his story.

Meditation

Find a comfortable position....Close your eyes....Roll your shoulders, releasing the tension....Take a deep breath....Let it out slowly....Whisper, "Jesus."....Relax....Look into life's reflection....Look at yourself....

You are sitting in front of a campfire....Sparks from the fire fly around your head, popping and cracking....Smoke slowly raises it head, floating into the crisp night air....Listen carefully. Crickets sing the last notes of their late summer symphony, their voices soon to be stilled by the cold night air of fall and winter....Jesus is on his haunches warming his hands by the fire....The disciples are gathered closely together at the fire's edge attempting to wrap themselves in the warmth of the burning wood....Jesus looks up from the fire and calls out your name....He pats the ground, inviting you to sit down next to him....Move quickly to his side....A smile brightens Jesus' face. "I am so glad that you are here tonight," he says patting you on the back....His hand lingers....A warmth spreads its fingers across your shoulders and down your spine....Peter is finishing the last bites of supper, stopping only to wipe the remains from his full red beard....James pokes at the fire with a stick, sending popping sparks into the night air....

"Let me tell you a story about buried treasure, and let's see if you can tell me what the treasure is. Once upon a time, there were two men looking for a treasure....The first man went into a field and began digging holes all over the land....Finally, he found the buried treasure....The young man, about your age, lifted the treasure from its earth-filled grave, wiping away the dirt and rocks....Then, looking around to make sure that no one saw him, he opened the treasure and peeked inside....The treasure was much too valuable to keep in his house, so he found a new hiding place. 'What if someone else finds my treasure?' he thought to himself. So the young man went out and sold everything that he owned....Then he took the money and bought the field where his treasure was buried. Now he truly owned the treasure.

"The second man was a shopkeeper who sold only the finest pearls. The white-haired man searched the world over for the most perfect pearl....After many years of searching and buying and selling pearls, he found the most perfect pearl of them all. The old man was very happy—but he found that the pearl cost a great deal of money. He went back home and counted all of his coins, but there was only one way he could ever buy the perfect pearl....He sold everything that he owned: his house, his clothes, his jewels, his land....At last, he was able to buy the pearl."

Jesus stands and stretches his arms and legs....A low murmuring of the disciples cuts through the chill of evening.... Wrap your coat tightly around your shoulders....Jesus turns to you. He asks, "My friend, what treasure am I talking about?"....Answer Jesus. (*Pause briefly.*) Jesus sits once again, shifting his feet in the sandy soil, then explains: "The kingdom of heaven is like the buried treasure and the fine pearl....Would you understand this better if we were talking about BMWs, trips around the world, or beautiful people? The two men were willing to give up everything they had in order to make the treasure their own....If you want a ticket into God's kingdom, you better decide on a few things in your life that you are willing to 'sell'—to give up." (*Pause.*)

The disciples gather together, discussing Jesus' lesson....You are all alone with Jesus, enjoying the comfort of the warm fire and the time with Jesus....Tell him of those things that are of greatest importance to you....Is it the people in your life?.... Are your friends of more importance than your family? (*Pause briefly.*) Is doing everything "your way" more important than pleasing others? (*Pause briefly.*) A question forms upon your lips....As though reading your thoughts, Jesus responds, "I know the biggest question you have: 'What do I have to give up?'."....I will leave you alone to talk this over with Jesus. (*Pause for approximately one minute or until they grow restless.*)

Prayer

Lord, I come before you with my own set of values, some good, some not worthy of you. By your example teach me the value of God's kingdom. Help me to find the right order in my value system. Strengthen my walk with you, Lord. Amen.

It is time to leave Jesus' side....Feel his strong arms around you....Turn away from the hiss and spew of the campfire.... Walk down the weed-covered path....Open your eyes and return to this room.

Discussion

Pass out paper and pencils. Depending on the number of students, you may wish to break down into several small groups. Display the first list of valuables made in class. Place the answer choices for questions two, three, and four on the board or newsprint. Take time to answer each question yourself and share your answer with the group; thus you can model the time allotted for responding.

1. Take a look at the list of things you would buy if you came into sudden wealth. Now assume that your home is on fire. You have one minute to run through the house and gather all of the things of value in your life. Be very specific; don't just name "CD"s or items that represent your church.

Give them about a minute and a half to compose their lists.

Now share your list and why you made these choices with those in your group.

2. Take one more look at the list of items saved from the fire and make a decision which of these items:

• will be of value to you in eight years: mark with "X."

• would affect your life if you lost them: mark with "+."

Share your response with your group. Be sure to tell why you chose what you did.

3. Now compare your list of those things you would buy if you found treasure and your list of valuables saved from the fire. What do your lists tell you? (*If no answers are forthcoming, suggest responses below.*)

• My values will change seriously in the future.

• My values will always be important.

• My list centers on... (e.g., myself, people, money, possessions, etc.).

4. If you were to make a comparison between those things you deem important and the value of your relationship with

Jesus, what would your reaction be? (*If no answers are forthcoming, suggest responses below.*)

- I'm in trouble now.
- No problem.
- Maybe if....
- First things first.

Closing

Leader: Thank you, Lord, for this time together.

Stand together in a circle, holding hands. Pray the Our Father.

The Successful Picnic

Scripture: Mt 14:13-21
Feast: Seventeenth Sunday in Ordinary Time (B)
    Eighteenth Sunday in Ordinary Time (A)
Suggested Music: *Dreamland* or "We Believe in
    You"/*Instruments of Peace*

Where might we find you if you were given a whole day to relax and let the troubles of the world go by? Would your plans include feeding five thousand people? Probably not.

Jesus took a day off to relax and unwind. His day off suddenly turned into a very large picnic. Let's release our imaginations to see how Jesus and his disciples handled the unexpected picnic.

Meditation

Find a comfortable position....Close your eyes....Let your arms grow heavy, falling to your side....Take a deep breath....Let it out slowly....Whisper, "Jesus."....

You are standing in a grassy meadow....The tall blades of grass sway in the gentle summer breeze....Wild flowers peak from within the green leaves of spring....The blue waters of the Sea of Galilee stretch as far as your eye can see....Jesus sits quietly in a small wooden boat....The rushing waters slap at the side of the vessel, pushing it back and forth at will....Peter throws a rope toward you....Grab the rope, pulling until it stings your hands....The bow heads into the waiting shoreline, crunching on the sandy bar....A saddened Jesus steps out of the boat. Reaching out, he takes your hand....You steady his uncertain steps....Smiling, he wraps his arms about you, not saying a word....With the blink of his eyes, tears are

159

pushed downward on his weary cheek....Wipe away his tears
with the back of your hand....Look at your hand in the
sunlight....The tears, the sorrow of Jesus, are held within your
hand....Jesus, speaks softly, offering an explanation, "My
cousin, John, the one who baptized me, has been put to death
by King Herod."....You see his pain....Take a moment and
comfort Jesus. (*Pause briefly.*)

The disciples climb quietly out of the bobbing boat, making
their way through the damp sand....They join you and Jesus
on the path....John, wiping his sand-caked feet, notices the
large crowd that has gathered to meet Jesus...."Lord, these
people have walked miles around the water's edge to see
you."....Jesus sighs, rests his hand on your shoulder, and
begins walking toward the growing crowd....He steps among
the people, blessing and healing the sick....A small boy leaning
on a wooden crutch, his leg wrapped in cloth bandages,
reaches out to touch Jesus....Jesus gently places his hand on
the sick child's head and then moves on....The startled boy
throws down his crutch, walking with an uneven gait, then
leaps for joy....The swelling crowd crushes forward....Standing
on an outcropping of rock you view the wall of people....
Jesus, your Lord, sees their pain....He moves swiftly through
the milling crowd, offering God's blessing to all.

The sun begins its slumber....Only a soft glow remains on the
meadow....Peter pushes his way through the throng....
Breathlessly he tells Jesus, "We have been talking, Lord. It is
growing late. We must send these people on their way. We
cannot feed ourselves, let alone this crowd!"....Jesus turns
sharply, looking at Peter, "There is no need to send them
away....Gather the food together and feed the people."....
Jesus resumes his walk among the people....Peter's mouth
drops open....For once he is left speechless....Peter walks off
muttering to himself....Jesus turns to you, "Help Peter gather
the food....Place all that you find beneath those trees."....Take
the empty basket from Thomas....Weave through the
multitude....Notice a small child motioning to you....The child
hands you his small basket of bread and dried fish...."This is all

that I have, but you may share this with Jesus," the child tells you....This pathetic amount of food is all you can find....Reach into the small knapsack tied around your waist....Pull out the bread you were saving and place it in the basket....

Join the disciples, placing the gathered food at Jesus' feet....Count the loaves of bread. "One, two, three, four, five loaves of bread and two fish is all that we have. This will never be enough," Peter once again cautions...."Invite the people to spread blankets on the grass and prepare to share a meal," Jesus orders....Jesus raises the food above his head, offering God a prayer of thanksgiving....He hands the bread to Timothy, "Pass this out to the people."....Timothy breaks off hunks of bread, passing it to waiting hands....Jesus turns to you, handing you a fish...."Share this with our friends."....Walk among the sea of faces....Break off pieces of the fish....Share them with the grateful people....When the last person is fed, join Jesus sitting beneath the golden-yellow trees....Jesus shares his food with you, breaking the bread and fish into pieces....Jesus smiles, "When I have a picnic, I really have a picnic, don't I?"....You share the meal and laughter with Jesus....

"Gather the leftovers and bring them to me," Jesus tells the disciples....Grab an empty basket....Return to Jesus with the gathered leftovers....The disciples place their overflowing baskets next to yours....There are twelve baskets of bread and fish left over!....Jesus takes note of your expression of disbelief....

"Come and join me, my friend," Jesus invites....Settle yourself on the fallen tree...."Why are you surprised that we have leftovers? God always give us more than we can use. There is more sunshine than we can ever see....Look out at the grass covering the meadow. We cannot count the blades of grass. There are more roaring rivers and babbling brooks than we can ever hear....There are more trees reaching their arms to the heavens than you can climb....You have more clothing than you can wear at one time....God is good to us, so do not be surprised that we have enough food to eat....When God gives us anything, he makes sure we have enough, and some left over."

Jesus stands, stretches out his arms as far as possible, and says laughing, "God loves you this much."....You smile, remembering the early days of childhood....Jesus takes your hand in his, "You were blessed with many special gifts that will help feed the needs of the world....I need your gifts....I need you to walk beside me."....I will leave you alone with Jesus for your response....

Prayer

Jesus, most of the time I fail to stop and count my blessings. I often complain, wanting more. May your Holy Spirit strengthen me to share God's blessings and love with others. Amen.

It is time to leave Jesus and the picnic behind....Reach into your pocket and give Jesus something that you brought with you today....something that you treasure. (*Pause briefly.*) Stand; walk through the green meadow....Open your eyes and return to this room.

Discussion

- If you had been with the disciples when Jesus ordered you to feed the people, what would you have done?

- What is the lesson to be learned in this story?

- Is God calling you to "feed the people"? How does this make you feel?

Closing

Standing together in oneness and unity, pray the Lord's Prayer in echo format, inviting as many voices as feel called to echo your lead.

Jesus and Peter Take a Walk

Scripture: Mt 14:22-33
Feast: Nineteenth Sunday in Ordinary Time (A)
Suggested Music: *The Sea* **or "By Name I Have Called You"/*Gentle Sounds***

Has trusting someone ever put you in a difficult situation? What happened? Were you able to trust this person again? Why or why not?

In times of moral or physical danger it often becomes difficult to reach out in absolute faith. For a moment, place yourself in a small fishing boat being tossed about like a cork in a bathtub. A person that you have known only for a short time tells you to step out of the boat and *walk* across the storm-ravaged sea, the depth of which goes well beyond the reach of sunlight. What is your answer?

Peter, rough and coarse by most people's standards, was given just such a command. Let's release our imaginations to join Peter and Jesus on a stormy sea.

Meditation

Find a comfortable position....Close your eyes....Roll your shoulders, releasing the cares of today....Take a deep breath....Let it out slowly....Whisper, "Jesus."....Relax....

You are sitting beside a lake....Early evening whispers its shadows across the sea....Lake waters lap at the shore....Take a few deep breaths....Smell the cool fresh air....Several small

fishing boats float upon the calm green water....Fishermen
return to shore....Several hundred feet down the shoreline,
Jesus and his disciples are stepping into a boat....Call out to
Jesus....He looks up, then recognizes you, calling your name.
"Would you like to come with us?" he adds....Run down the
water's edge....Your feet sink into the muddy mire....Cold, wet
sand seeps up through your toes as you run....

Jesus looks very tired, but he is smiling at you...."Help Peter
push out into the water," he tells you....Peter's red, scraggly
beard outlines his weathered face...."Push as hard as you
can," Peter tells you....The boat struggles against the return to
sea....At long last the boat frees itself from the sandy muck....
Hop on board....Your foot drags through the cool water....The
soft breeze of evening blows through your hair....Jesus moves
over, making room for you to join him...."Row the boat to the
opposite side of the lake," he tells the men....Moonlight
streaks the water with its yellow haze, offering a sense of
direction....When at last you reach the other shore, a large
purple mountain rises above the water, casting its dark shadow
over the boat....Jesus announces that he is going to climb the
mountain and pray to his Father....Stepping out of the boat,
he waves goodbye, instructing the disciples to come back later.

As the boat leaves Jesus and the shore behind, you feel the
gentle rolling of the waves beneath the boat....Lay your head
back against the seat to rest....Hear the soft murmuring of the
disciples' voices; it is time to return to the shore for Jesus....In
the yellow glow of moonlight, the mountain's shadow grows
smaller....The air suddenly stirs around you, blowing your
hair....Water sprays across your face....A sudden windstorm
propels the small boat across the sea....Look around you....
James's hands grip the oars, his knuckles white....The
sleeping disciples are tossed about in the bottom of the boat
like rag dolls....Peter shouts, "The winds are pushing us
further out!....We won't be able to go back and pick up
Jesus."....All the disciples are awake now, pulling on the oars,
but the small boat does not make any headway....

In the direction of the distant shore a strange figure appears above the lake....It moves slowly, on top of the water, toward the boat...."It's a ghost!" the disciples cry....A shiver goes down your spine...."Let me out of here!" one of the disciples cries into the night....You peek over the railing of the boat, afraid to see and more afraid not to see the strange happenings...."How can this be?" you ask no one in particular....From the shifting waters and fog-shrouded lake you hear, "Do not be afraid! It is I, Jesus."....The figure makes its way through the foamy sea....Peer into the fog....It is Jesus!....The skeptical disciples take turns calling out, "Who are you?"....Peter stands on the bow of the boat, his hair pulled back by the force of the wind, calling out, "If that is you, Lord, tell me to come to you on the water."

Beyond the fog, beyond the cold spray of water, the soft but demanding voice of Jesus fills the night air, "Peter, come to me." Peter hesitates, looking at the other men, then climbs out of the boat, stepping onto the cold, dark waters....Waves and wind pound the boat....Peter begins to sink....Winds howl...."I am afraid! Help me, Lord!" Peter cries in fear.... Jesus reaches out his hand to Peter, "Oh, you of little faith.... Why did you doubt me?" Jesus asks Peter....Jesus holds Peter's hand in his, walking toward the boat....Suddenly, Jesus stops and calls your name...."Come to me, my friend."....Jesus holds out his arms....Waves buffet the boat....I will leave you alone to decide if you are going to step out of the boat onto the water. (Pause.) Tell Jesus how you feel....

When Jesus and Peter climb back into the boat, the wind stops....The waters are stilled....There is silence everywhere.... You are only aware of the sound of your own heartbeat....The disciples fall on their knees...."Truly, you are the son of God!"...."May God's blessing be with you of faith," he tells everyone....

Jesus settles back against the bow of the boat once again.... Rest your head against his chest....Listen to Jesus' heart.... Place your hand on your own heart....Feel the rhythm; the two hearts beat as one...."Asking you to get out of the boat was a test, you know," Jesus whispers...."If you could measure your faith, is there enough to see you through the bad days? (*Pause.*) Where in your life am I inviting you to 'get out of the boat'?....Friends, school, work, home, future plans, your commitment to me?" (*Pause.*)

Prayer

Jesus, there are times I don't even know what faith means. There are fears that come in the dark of life and I forget to turn to you. Fill me with the strength of your faith. Steady my walk with you. Amen.

It is time to return to shore and say goodbye to Jesus....Step out of the boat....Walk up the sandy path....Turn and wave one last goodbye....Open your eyes and return to this room.

Discussion

- Why would Peter tell Jesus, "If that is you, Lord, tell me to come to you on the water"?

- Was Jesus angry or upset with Peter?

- If you were in Peter's shoes and Jesus made you the same invitation, how would you respond?

- Is Jesus inviting you to "get out of the boat" in some area of your life?

Closing

You may want to play background music and use candlelight to set the mood.

Invite the teens to give silent reflection to their answer to the last question:

- What is your response to Jesus' invitation to "get out of the boat"?

- Are you willing to take that first step out of the boat?

33. Jesus and Peter Take a Walk

Leader: Lord, Peter had the strength to test his faith. My legs
are weak; my spirit, unsure. I am uncertain of things I
do not know. Strengthen my walk with you, O Lord.

*Ask for prayer petitions and have the teens respond, "Lord,
hear my prayer."*

Close with a group Glory Be to the Father.

The Banquet Feast

Scripture: Lk 14:1,7-14
Feast: Twenty-Second Sunday in Ordinary Time (C)
Suggested Music: *Dreamland*

For the moment, let's say that this is your birthday (*select several students*). Whom would you invite to your party? Do you want to invite a famous person? Would you want to invite someone who would make you look good? Do you ask someone who you know will bring an expensive present? What would happen if the invited guests failed to show? How do you feel when someone turns down your invitation to a party? If Jesus were to give a party, whom do you think that he would invite? (*Allow for a variety of answers and include the poor, the sick, the lonely, etc.*)

One day Jesus was invited to a dinner party. Many of the invited guests had failed to show. The ones who were there were squabbling among themselves, for they all wanted to sit next to Jesus in the place of honor. So he told them a story. Let's release our imaginations, recalling a time long ago.

Meditation

Find a comfortable position....Close your eyes....Shut out the noises around you....Relax....Take a deep breath....Let it out slowly and whisper, "Jesus."....

Waiters scurry about the room with huge trays of food....Smell the roast turkey, the gravy, the potatoes....The table is heavy with food....Take a seat around the long table....Jesus smiles and welcomes you to the party....Jesus stands, looking at all the guests pushing and shoving to sit next to him.... Seeing this, he tells a story....

"Once a upon a time a king threw a big party for his son's birthday. The prince was going to be sixteen years old. His father told him that he could invite anyone he wanted to his party. The prince said to himself, 'I want some decent presents, so I'll invite a lot of people, especially rich ones. The prince did not invite Kirk because he was a laughingstock. Everyone made fun of him because he walked with a limp. The prince did not invite Brian because Brian's parents were very poor and the prince did not like to be seen with 'that kind of person.' The prince did not invite Roberto because he was different, and besides Roberto never invited him to any parties."....

The room grows silent as Jesus walks to the end of the table, to the seat next to you....As Jesus takes his seat he asks, "Whom was the prince thinking about when he made out his guest list?"....Jesus then continues, "The next time you have a party, ask people who probably are never asked to a party. Ask people who can't invite you to their party because they cannot afford to even buy a cake. Ones to whom food is luxury."....Upon hearing this, the host calls his servants: "Go out into the streets and bring in the poor, the crippled, the blind, and the lame. My house will be full. My honored guests have dishonored me with their absence."....Jesus smiles to himself, then adds, "If you do this, you will surely be rewarded for being so kind."....The dinner guests lower their heads sheepishly, ashamed for how they have acted....The host quickly orders the servant to form a big circle with the tables. That way no one has a better seat than anyone else....The food is passed and the party begins....

Following the meal, Jesus asks you to join him in the courtyard....The sweet smell of roses and lilacs fills the night air....Jesus sits down on the porch swing, inviting you to join him...."I want you to remember my story. God does not have favorite people. God's circle of love is offered to everyone."....
The moonlight casts shadows across the fragrant gardens....
Jesus places his arm around your shoulders, then asks, "The

banquet of which I speak is God's kingdom. Those who failed to answer the invitation were too busy with other things— things of no importance."....Jesus pauses for a cool drink of water, then continues, "Do you ever think that you are better than someone else?"....Selecting a blossom from the rose bush, he asks, "If my Father invited you to spend some time with him, what would you answer?"....I will leave you with Jesus to talk this over.

Prayer

Jesus, forgive me for those times I think only of my own importance. Let me live as you did, humbly serving God, treating others with love and respect. Help me count all others as no less important or more important to you than myself. Amen.

It is time to leave....Tell Jesus goodbye....Turn and walk through the garden gate....Open your eyes and return to this room.

Discussion

- What would it take for you to accept an invitation to spend some time with God?

- If you accepted God's invitation, what would you expect in return: (*e.g., would all your future needs would be met?; would your life be carefree and without doubt or worry?*).

- What might God ask of you?

Jesus Cures the Deaf

Scripture: Mk 7:31-37
Feast: Twenty-Third Sunday in Ordinary Time (B)
Suggested Music: *Dream Journey* or "Healer of Our Every
    Ill"/*Instruments of Peace*

Does anyone have a family member or perhaps a friend who is deaf? Can you imagine life without sound? Most of us take our hearing for granted, choosing to be selective about the sounds that are irritating to us. The deaf have no choice in the matter. They cannot hear the sound of rain in a forest, the music of a rolling surf, the laughter of children at play, happy sounds, or sad sounds. The deaf are given few choices: get a hearing aid, learn to read lips, or not communicate with anyone. Jesus dealt with deafness in a different manner. Perhaps he wasn't just talking about not hearing with our ears. Let's release our imaginations and see how Jesus responded when a deaf man asked for help.

Meditation

Find a comfortable position....Close your eyes....Allow your muscles to relax....Move your head from side to side...Take a deep breath....Whisper, "Jesus."....Relax

This day finds that you have walked many miles across the hot desert sands....Dirt is caked upon your feet....Sit down by the side of the road....Take off your shoes....Wipe your feet with your hand; particles of gravel and sand once again take their place upon the earth....Many others travel this road: the old and bent, the young, the ill, and the lame....They are all following the path of Jesus. You have little to complain about....People from nearby villages have heard that Jesus has arrived near the Sea of Galilee....Look over your shoulder.... Below the hillside, waters of the sea kiss the shore....Make you way to the water's edge....Dip your feet in the cool waters.... You feel the touch of a hand upon your shoulder....Look up.... It is Jesus....He smiles broadly; leaning on your shoulder for support, he lowers himself to the ground....He removes his sandals....Sitting on the shore, Jesus dips his feet in the chilling water....Suddenly refreshed, and with a twinkle in his eye, he playfully splashes water on you....Jesus chuckles, then picking up his sandals, he rises to his feet....Many villagers have gathered on the hillside behind you...."Come, my friend, it is time for me to return to the people....Dry your feet off," Jesus says, handing you a small towel from his waist...Walk beside him up the sloping hillside to the waiting mass of people....

Wait for Jesus in the shade of a large rose bush....One by one, he patiently blesses each one, always showing his love and kindness to all....A small band of four men and two women attempt to break through the crowd, shouting, "Jesus! Jesus! Help this poor man!"....Jesus seems not to notice the demands of this group....Peter urges the crowd to let them through....The woman dressed in a dark blue veil pushes a sad-looking little man toward Jesus....The little man trembles at the sight of Jesus, falling upon his knees...."Help him, Jesus. He cannot hear a word, and he speaks very little....He has been this way since birth."...."You are his last hope. Help him, Jesus," begs another....Jesus looks with pity on this poor little man; a tear falls to Jesus' cheek....He looks out at the crowd crying out for his healing touch....Jesus takes the deaf man's hand and leads him to where you are sitting, away from the clamor and noise.

Jesus places his hand on the frail man's ears, then he places his fingers on his own tongue and touches the deaf man's ears....Jesus looks up to heaven and with a deep sigh says, "Ephphatha!" which means "Be opened!"....The once-frozen face of the little man jerks with excitement....He turns his head to the right and to the left, listening to the sounds of life for the first time....Turning to the crowd, he shouts, "I can hear!"....He kisses the hand of Jesus, "Thank you, Lord. You truly are the son of God."....The crowd cheers the name of Jesus...."Thanks be to God," shouts the crowd....An echo repeats itself across the hillside, "Jesus, Jesus."....The now unruly crowd gathers the little man up and places him high upon their shoulders; they walk triumphantly toward their homes in the nearby villages....

Jesus looks tired but happy. "Let's rest for a while," he suggests....You and Jesus make your way back to the seaside....It is almost evening....The sun begins to fall beyond the walls of the sea....Jesus dabbles his feet in the cool water....Circles of minnows play beneath the water....Turning to you, Jesus asks, "How often do you turn a deaf ear to God, my friend? (*Pause.*) Have you been able to hear my call? Do you even care if I call?" (*Pause.*) Jesus places the palm of his hand on your back, and asks, "What can I do for you, my friend?"....I will leave you for a moment to speak with Jesus.

Prayer

Jesus, when anger fills my heart, my ears close to you. When I fail to serve another, my ears close to you. Open my spirit that I may hear. Move within my heart that I may serve and love others. Bless my lips that I may speak your words. Amen.

It is time to say goodbye to Jesus now....Get up and walk away....Turn and wave once more....Open your eyes and return to this room.

Discussion

- Why would Jesus choose this method of healing? (*The people of Jesus' day believed that healing powers were within saliva. Observing animals licking their wounds, the people concluded that if saliva promoted healing in an animal it would also be helpful with a human. They*

*thought that saliva could be helpful in curing many
different kinds of illness, including deafness.)*

- If you could take a guess, what were the deaf man's first words?

- What do you think the deaf man may have done with the rest of his life?

- If you were healed by Jesus, what would you do with the rest of your life?

- Are there people in your life who have cared enough to take you to the side of Jesus? Who? How?

Closing

*Invite prayers of petition and have the teens respond,
"Lord, hear our prayer."*

Leader: Thank you, Lord, for this time of healing. We pray for
those who do not hear your words. We pray for those
who cannot speak your blessings. Touch their lives
with your love. Help us to be aware of those who feel
separated and alone because of their disabilities. Amen.

Forgive and Forgive Again

Scripture: Mt 18:21-35
Feast: Twenty-Fourth Sunday in Ordinary Time (A)
Suggested Music: *Bamboo Waterfall* or "Pardon Your
    People"/*Gentle Sounds*

Forgiving someone who has repeatedly hurt you is extremely difficult for everyone. Many times this happens within a family. Brothers or sisters may try to set you up to get into trouble with your parents, or worse. It hurts and creates anger when it is a friend or a person whom you trust, but many times the anger/hurt is so much more intense when the hurt has come from your own family. Getting even just becomes an endless cycle with no winners.

What is the worst thing that a brother or sister has ever done to you?

Sometimes I wonder how many times I have to forgive. It just seems that if there is any justice then I should be able to not offer forgiveness. In the days of Jesus, the Jews believed that your obligation to forgive consisted of three times. If the offender did it the fourth time, you did not need to forgive him.

One day Peter asked Jesus how often he must forgive someone. Probably thinking that he all ready knew the answer—three times—Peter was in for a shock. He undoubtedly thought that he was being very generous suggesting seven times. Jesus responded to Peter by telling a story. Perhaps we should listen to the story. It might even give us a different view on forgiveness.

Meditation

Find a comfortable position....Close your eyes....Roll your shoulders, releasing all the tension....Take a deep breath....Let it out slowly....Whisper, "Jesus."....Relax....

You are seated in the dining area of a small house....The walls are made of uneven bricks of dried mud....Jesus sits at the head of the table....Candles dismiss their flickering light to dance across the room....Peter sits on Jesus' right, slowly running his fingers through his red beard....Jesus smiles, popping a grape into his mouth....You start to say something to Jesus but Peter interrupts, asking, "Lord, how many times do I forgive someone who has really yanked my chain?"....Peter smugly leans back in his chair suggesting, "Up to seven times?"....Jesus shakes his head, "Not seven times, but seventy times seven."....You ponder the mathematics, wishing your calculator was in your pocket....Seven times seven is forty-nine; seven times seventy is 490 times!....Peter blusters, suggesting that Jesus had made an error....Jesus gently directs Peter to listen for a change...."Let me tell you a story that will explain what I mean."

You settle back on one elbow, propping a pillow behind your back....Jesus leans forward, "The kingdom of heaven is like a king who wanted to settle his accounts with his servants. The first servant owed the king millions of dollars. The king learned that the servant had no way of paying the money back, so he ordered the servant and his wife and his children and all that he had be sold to repay the debt. The servant fell on his knees, begging, 'Give me another chance; I will pay back what I owe you.' The king, feeling sorry for his servant, forgave the debt and sent the servant on his way. The servant quickly ran out the door and down the road. But on his way, he met one of his fellow servants, who owed him a few dollars. He grabbed him by the neck and began to choke him. 'Pay back what you owe me!' he demanded. 'Be patient; I will pay you back all that I owe,' the man begged. But the first servant refused. Instead he had the poor man thrown into prison until he could pay the debt. When the other servants saw this they told the king what had happened. The king called the servant in. 'You are wicked,' he told the servant, 'I forgave your debt because you begged me to. Shouldn't you have mercy on your fellow servant just as I had on you?' The king was very angry and turned the servant over to jailers to be tortured until he could pay back all he owed."....Jesus rests his elbows on the wooden table. Speaking in a low but firm voice he continues, "This is how my heavenly Father will treat each one of you unless you forgive your brother from your heart."....Peter, seeking the last word, interrupts, "Now, Jesus, let's take another look at this,"....His words hang in mid-air....Jesus places a finger over his mouth, "Shhh! I said listen, not argue."....

One by one the disciples leave the table to talk among themselves, for indeed Jesus has given them food for thought....Jesus gathers bread crumbs in his hand; turning toward the small window, he throws the small morsels to the birds....Jesus places his hand on your shoulder and says, "Once and for all, I want you to understand that you are always forgiven by God. He asks in return for you to be ready to forgive someone else....You can never out-forgive God."....A low murmur of voices drifts into the room...."They need to think a while on this one," he says explaining the debate going on...."Let's walk outside so that we can talk," Jesus directs.... Moonlight interrupts the darkness of night....Jesus turns to you once again, "Whom do you really need to forgive? Is there a constant battle going on inside you because of this? Do you wake up angry some mornings and go to bed hurt and upset?"....Jesus walks to the well, pulls the bucket up for water, and offers you the cup...."I am going to ask again. Is there someone you need to forgive?"....I will leave you alone with Jesus to talk about this. (*Pause until they become restless.*)

The cool, crisp fall air sends a chill down your back....Jesus pulls a roughly woven blanket around your shoulders....Take a portion of the cloth and place it over his lap....He smiles, pats you on the hand, then speaks, "Pretending that you are the only one wronged only causes more stress and confusion. The most healing act we can perform for ourselves is to ask for both God's forgiveness and to be forgiven by those we may have wronged. Is there someone whom you need to ask for forgiveness?" (*Pause.*) You are still alone with Jesus.

Prayer

Heavenly Father, at times my anger overcomes my judgment. May your love be a constant reminder to forgive and to be forgiven. Amen.

Discussion

- Why do you think Peter asked Jesus how many times he needed to forgive?

- Who is the hardest person for you to forgive? Why?

- Who has continuously forgiven you? Why?

Closing

Leader: Lord, we have come together to share your forgiveness. Be with us as we walk into the world of conflicts and temptations. I am sorry, Lord, for all those things which I have chosen to do and not to do. May God's blessings be upon my enemies. Amen.

The Grateful Leper

Scripture: Lk 17:11-19
Feast: Twenty-Eighth Sunday in Ordinary Time (C)
**Suggested Music: *Bamboo Waterfall* or "We Believe in
    You"/*Gentle Sounds***

Did your parents make you write "thank you" notes after
birthday parties or Christmas? Do you still take time to write
them? But perhaps we should turn the situation around. How
many times have you done something really nice for someone,
and you never heard a word of thanks from them? It makes
you wonder if all the efforts were worthwhile, doesn't it? I
would imagine that the two people in our lives whom we really
take for granted are Mom and Dad. How many times have
you said to your mother or father, "Thanks for going to work
today so I can have a pair of soccer shoes," or "Thanks for the
food on the table"? Over and over we seem to move through
our lives always expecting to be on the receiving end.

Did Jesus ever experience what it was like when people forgot
to say thank you? When?

One day in particular, Jesus found out what it was like when
people forget to say thank you. He was on his way to Jerusalem
when he encountered ten people who had leprosy. (*You may
want to explain that untreated leprosy consists of open
sores on the skin, often resulting in disfigurement. Leprosy
is very contagious and people with leprosy were banned
from entering the villages. They were to never touch
another person, required to announce, "Unclean! Unclean!"
when others were within eyesight. The were completely
rejected by the people.*) Let's release our imagination, joining
Jesus on the road between Galilee and Samaria.

Meditation

Find a comfortable position....Close your eyes....Allow your arms to fall limp at your side....Take a deep breath....Let it out slowly....Whisper, "Jesus."....Relax....Look into the mirror of life....The reflection is yours....

Your feet are covered with gritty sand and particles of rock surrendered by the high mountains surrounding the valley....Jesus and his disciples have invited you to join them on their journey....The road winds endlessly in the distance....Peter, grumbling as usual, mumbles, "We must be somewhere between Samaria and Galilee, but God knows why."....Dirt clouds billow around your feet....The trek has been slow and long....Winter winds whip across the lands....People hearing that Jesus is nearby flock to the roadway, hoping to catch sight of him and often pleading for his healing touch....John, the youngest disciple, walks beside you....Suddenly he stops in his tracks, signaling for the party to halt....John points a shaking finger toward a group of people standing huddled together against the cold....Look ahead....There they are— men, women, and young people about your age....They are covered with rotting bandages....Peter warns, "These people are lepers! Watch out!"....Observe the young people.... Weeping, open sores cover their faces and hands....Dark ugly circles form half moons under their eyes....Sunken cheeks and swollen bellies tell of hunger and pain....Mark places his hand on your shoulder reassuring you, "They won't come near. It is against the law."....The lepers reach for their rag-torn clothing to cover their faces....One of the lepers calls out to Jesus.... "Are you the one who breathes life into the dying?"....Jesus nods his head, but remains silent...."We beg for your mercy. We are walking death. There is no place to call home; there are no meals waiting for us."....Jesus walks to the edge of the road but does not step any closer....You hand Jesus a cloth to cover his nose against the smell of rotting flesh. It is then that you see tears upon Jesus' cheeks...."Please, Jesus, help them," you whisper....Jesus calls out to the lepers, "I will help you, but first you must go and show yourself to your priest."....Peter, always quick with the whys and wheres, offers, "According to the law, priests are supposed to check over those who have this disease. They will decide if these outcasts are healed."....

The ten lepers run toward the village....Jesus says very little, placing his hand upon your shoulder as you continue your journey....You walk in silence, thinking only of the sight you have just witnessed....You question why these people paid the price of pain and suffering....As you approach the village gate, two men standing nearby are talking about the lepers. "Yes, I saw them with my own eyes! I was terrified at first that they would actually come into our village. They were all shouting, 'We are healed!'....Their skin was clear and free of sores. The odor was gone."....Jesus smiles quietly to himself....A man in the distance breaks into a run, waving his arms in the air. He is unrecognizable except for his torn and dirty clothing. Bandages fall to the ground as he runs....Quickly he comes to Jesus' side....The man, in his early twenties, stands straight and tall, then falls to his knees shouting praise and thanks to God...."God is my strength. Thank you, Jesus, for giving me back my life."...Jesus takes the man's hands in his, saying, "You are welcome, but weren't there ten people healed?"....Jesus turns back toward you and the disciples, asking, "Where are the other nine?"....Peter buries his cold hands in the folds of his cloak, "Only one bothered to come back, Jesus," he growls....Jesus helps the man to his feet, speaking lovingly, "Stand and go. Your faith has made you well."....The grateful man slowly turns away and heads toward the Samaritan village he once called home.

"That really takes the cake. Only one bothers to tell Jesus thanks," mutters Peter....Jesus pats Peter on the back, then continues walking toward the village well....His shoulders sag with weariness....A veil of sadness covers his face....You look down the road, then say to Jesus, "Maybe the others had further to go and they will come along any time now."....Jesus shakes his head, then speaks slowly, "Always be grateful for the things that God does for you. God usually sends these blessings our way through other people. You must take the time to recognize a gift when it is given."....Leaning against the wall surrounding the well, Jesus imparts his wisdom once again, "Take time to tell God 'thank you.' How do you think he feels when you fail to thank him for all he has done for you? God does notice and so do the people closest to you."....

I will leave you alone....In the silence, give thanks for all the blessings in your own life....Think of all those you have taken for granted....

Prayer

Jesus, Jesus, my Lord, how do I begin to give thanks for your unconditional love? May I forgive as I have been forgiven. Allow me the grace to remember the people in my life and their efforts to make my life easier. Thank you for teaching that God cares for both our friends and our enemies. No one is outside the circle of his love. You give me hope; you give me life. Amen.

It is time for you to leave....Jesus places his arms around your shoulder, drawing you closer to him....Say goodbye....Turn and walk away....Open your eyes and return to this room.

Discussion

- What part did the lepers play in their own healing? Would you say the lepers had great faith, or were they just desperate?

- What do you think became of the grateful leper? Jesus told him, "Go on your way." What was Jesus talking about?

- Who are the "lepers" in your school? In your town? Do you have a good excuse for not reaching out to them?

Closing Prayer

Ask the students to give a few moments of thought to all of the blessings in their own lives, perhaps recognizing those people who, day after day, care enough to give the very best.

37. The Grateful Leper

Invite the young people to stand in a circle and suggest that each contribute a prayer of thanks for someone or for something in particular that God has given him/her. Have them respond, "I thank you, Lord," while extending their palms up.

Leader: We gather to give you thanks, Lord, for your gifts of love and forgiveness.

For the summer sun, the golden leaves of fall, the rush of winter winds, the newness of spring.

For the days of wonder, for the days of sadness, for the days of faith.

For the pleasure of friends, the love of family.

For the earth and her bounty, the rivers that flow, the trees that raise their arms in praise, the oceans that kiss the earth with power.

For all things big and small, spoken and unspoken, realized or to be realized.

Close with a group hug.

The Greatest Rule of All

Scripture: Mt 22:34-40
Feast: Thirtieth Sunday in Ordinary Time (A)
Suggested Music: "Peace Is Flowing Like a River"/*Gentle Sounds*

Invite each student to give his/her definition of love. More than likely, each will be different. Jot their definitions on the board or newsprint.

Most of us have our own ideas on the meaning of "love." The word covers a wide landscape of emotions and needs. We "love" chocolate ice cream. We "love" rap, jeans, cars (especially if they are ours), a cool mountain stream in the summertime, and the first snow of winter. How often do we say, "Man, do I love God"? Or how about this one: "I really love that guy down the street who let the air out of my tires"?

Think for a minute—are there people in your life whom you really love, and love unconditionally? I don't mean "like" or "would like to have a relationship with"—I mean love. Now think about bestowing this love on the homeless man who stands outside of Wal-Mart with a sign that reads, "I will work for food." Does the word still fit?

God has quite a bit to say about love. We tend to put his thoughts on the subject on the back burner, but within the pages of the Bible the message still stands. Jesus gave us two commandments to live by. One day a man of the law, thinking that he would trick Jesus, asked him which of God's commandments was the most important. Jesus surprised him with a simple answer—not the answer "ten" or "the 613 laws of the Pharisees." Free your imaginations, joining Jesus in the Temple courtyard.

Meditation

Find a comfortable position....Close your eyes....Roll your head from side to side, putting those neck muscles to rest....Take a deep breath....Let it out slowly....Whisper, "Jesus."....Relax

You find yourself with Jesus in the temple courtyard....Nearby an aged man calls out, "Doves for sale. Temple offering."....
Many people have gathered to hear what Jesus has to say—and to question his validity....Jesus motions for quiet....Seeing that the crowd has nearly pushed you into the Temple wall, Jesus reaches out, offering you his hand....Pulling you to his side, he says, "When I have finished here we will go someplace and talk....Wait right here for me."....Take a seat on the cushion next to Jesus....

A young man steps forward, demanding Jesus' attention....
"Jesus, which is the greatest commandment?" he asks....
There is a soft murmuring among the witnesses....Jesus thinks for a moment, then answers, "Love the Lord your God with your whole heart and your whole mind and your whole soul." Standing now in the place of honor, he goes on, "And the second is: Love your neighbor as yourself."....The young man seems puzzled by this answer, turning his back on Jesus....
Jesus looks at you saying, "Remember, my friend, you cannot love God without also loving your neighbor."

Jesus now steps down from the raised platform....Placing a hand on your shoulder, he directs you to a bench near the fountain....The cool spray from the fountain reminds you of a gentle summer rain....Sitting down, Jesus offers you a drink of water....Take a long drink; enjoy the clear, cool water...."I want you to remember that if you aren't able to love your brother or sister who is in your midst, then you may not be able to love the God whom you cannot see."

Jesus leans forward, resting his head in his hand. Turning toward you, he speaks softly: "Look into your own heart and think of the times that you have forgotten to love instead of teasing, harassing, tormenting, and ridiculing." Gazing at your reflection in the fountain, he asks, "My friend, how much time do you spend gossiping about your friends? (*Pause briefly.*) Do you turn your head away when you pass by the poor and the homeless? (*Pause briefly.*) Do you forget to say, 'I love you'? (*Pause briefly.*) Think on these things and then tell me how you will answer these questions."....I will leave you alone with Jesus for a moment. (*Pause for one minute or until they grow restless.*)

Prayer

Jesus, I talk a lot about love, often forgetting to share it with others. I do talk about my friends. I become angry, acting as though I am the only person with needs. Give me a gentle nudge when my will comes before yours. I do love you, Lord. Remind me to offer love rather than criticism to others. Amen.

It is time to leave....Tell Jesus goodbye....Walk through the courtyard....through the dense crowd of men weighing this simple commandment....Stop and wave....Open your eyes and return to this room.

Discussion

- When Jesus tells you to love God above all things with your total mind and body, what does that mean to you?

- If you tell someone that you "love" him/her, is this a commitment? Do you assume responsibility?

- Where do you find it the most difficult to offer God's love to others?

- When it comes to love, do actions speak louder than words?

Closing Prayer

Have the teens respond, "They will know we are Christians by our love." Optional: Sing the verses to "They Will Know We Are Christians by Our Love" as a response instead.

Hold hands, standing together in a circle.

Leader: For the teens across the land who face daily conflict, we offer our love. (*Response*)

Leader: For the children of this world, we offer our caring. (*Response*)

Leader: For the those who suffer the pain of AIDS, we offer our compassion. (*Response*)

Leader: For those imprisoned unfairly, we offer our justice. (*Response*)

Leader: For the homeless and the suffering, we offer our love. (*Response*)

Bartimaeus Sees the Light

Scripture: Mk 10:46-52
Feast: Thirtieth Sunday in Ordinary Time (B)
**Suggested Music: *Bamboo Waterfall* or "When You Seek
     Me"/*Gentle Sounds***

*Invite the group to spend a minute just looking around the
room. Then ask them to close their eyes. Now offer these
questions to think about.*

- What color is your sweater/shirt/blouse?

- Who is sitting on your right side?

- What color hair does the person in back of you have?

- What color shoes have I got on?

- Who is missing from our session today?

*Invite them to open their eyes and share how they did and
how they felt during the exercise.*

It must be very difficult to be blind, to never see children play,
to never see the colors of fall, to never be able to drive. The
list could go on and on. Most of us have the gift of sight and
yet how well do we use it? Like most things, we probably take
our sight for granted. One day while Jesus was walking
through the street of a city, he noticed a young, blind man
begging for food. When the man, called Bartimaeus, knew
that Jesus was nearby, he was relentless in getting Jesus'
attention. Release your imaginations, joining Jesus and the
blind man who never gave up.

Meditation

Take a comfortable position....Close your eyes....Roll your shoulders....Relax your arms and legs....Put all the sounds that you hear out of your mind....Take a deep breath....Let it out slowly....Whisper, "Jesus."....

You are with Jesus and his disciples outside the city of Jericho.... The roads are dusty with the tramping of feet.... Citizens push empty carts toward the marketplace....Others bring wagons loaded with lambs and chickens...."For Sale" signs hang limply on the side of the wooden stalls.... Children scramble past their parents, filled with excitement....This is a busy place....Peter rushes ahead to a cart filled with fresh fruits....He carefully chooses a bright red apple....Peter returns slowly, wiping the juice of the apple off his beard....James, sometimes the dreamer, brings a small handful of flowers from the street vendor....

Once through the gates of the city, you make your way through the narrow cobblestone streets....Each building is more beautiful than the last....Tall steeples reach toward the heavens....A young blind man sits among his tattered belongings begging for food...He is thin and frail....You wonder if he has ever had a bath....His skeletal frame is covered with rags....You turn to tell Jesus about the blind man, only to find that he has been nearly swallowed by the gathering crowd....The blind man calls out, "What is going on?"...."Jesus of Nazareth is here," you inform him....The blind man calls out to Jesus, "Jesus, son of David, have mercy on me!"....Jesus turns sharply, then calls you to his side.... "Who is that man?" he asks you....Before you can answer, a woman from the town replies, "That is just Bartimaeus, the town beggar."....Disgust lingers in the air...."Don't give him the time of day," shouts another....The crowd surges forward, separating you from Jesus....Surely he will help the blind man....

A soldier in the crowd tells Bartimaeus to quiet down....But the blind man calls out louder, "Son of David, have mercy on me!" Jesus stops and once again asks about this man....Jesus spots you, signaling for you to bring Bartimaeus to his side....

Bend low; whisper in Bartimaeus' ear....He jumps up quickly, spilling his small basket of coins....Take his hand; it is thin and fragile, his skin nearly transparent. Bartimaeus shakes with excitement....Lead him to Jesus' side....

Jesus reaches out, taking Bartimaeus' hands in his. "What do you want from me, my son?" he asks....Bartimaeus' eyes are clouded with darkness....He begs Jesus, "Grant that I may see the world with these eyes." Jesus looks squarely into the blank eyes and announces, "I am the light of the world."....Bending down to the ground, he mixes some saliva and dirt in his hand and makes mud out of it....Then he smears the mud over Bartimaeus' eyes....Jesus walks toward a fountain and washes his hands, telling Bartimaeus, "Come and wash the mud from your eyes."....Bartimaeus places his hand upon your shoulder....Lead him to the bubbling fountain....Pour the cool waters into his waiting hands....When the last spot of mud is washed clean, Bartimaeus opens his eyes.

The veil of blindness that once covered the man's eyes has disappeared....Bartimaeus' bright blue eyes reflect the light of day...."I can see! I can see!" he shouts out in joy....Jesus chuckles to himself....The crowd buzzes with excitement, crowding around the man they shunned a few moments before.

Jesus quickly leaves the crowd behind, leading you to the shelter of an olive grove....Wild flowers celebrate the day with bright blooms of color...."There is something that I want you to understand," Jesus tells you....Beneath the shade of the tree, move closer to Jesus....He places an arm around your shoulders...."I was sent into this world to make people see not only with their eyes but also with their hearts.".... "But why Bartimaeus?" you question...."Because he would not give up. In all of his darkness, with eyes that saw nothing, he knew that I was the Son of God. Bartimaeus was healed because he had faith and trust in me; he trusted God."....The gentle breath of summer blows Jesus' hair across his face. Jesus takes one hand and pulls his hair into a knot at the back of his head...."Being unable to see is not the only type of blindness. You can be blind to my love. You may not be able to see the way God works in your life."....Looking at you, he questions, "Do you know how much I love you?" (*Pause briefly.*) "What do you want me to do for you, my friend?"....

I will leave you in the olive grove with Jesus.

Prayer

Jesus, forgive me for those times that I fail to see the goodness in others; for the times I do not see the hand of God in my life; for failing to see the pain in others. Heal me, my Lord. Allow me to see more clearly. Amen.

The day has settled into evening....It is time for you to leave.... Walk down the path through the olive trees and retrace your steps to the gates of the city....Open your eyes and return to this room.

Discussion

- How did Jesus know that Bartimaeus truly recognized him as the Son of God? (*Bartimaeus called him the "son of David" although he thought that Joseph was Jesus' father.*)

- Has there been a miracle in your life? How did this affect your life?

- In what ways are your eyes closed? (*You may want to share first, setting the pace for the group.*)

Closing Prayer

We thank you God for lifting the veil of darkness from our eyes. Walk beside us as we make our way through this world. Amen.

Ask for prayers of petition and invite the teens to respond, "Lord, hear our prayers."

Leader: For these prayers and all those that are unspoken, we pray to the Lord. (*Response*)

Close with the Our Father.

Jesus Meets Zacchaeus

Scripture: Lk 19:1-10
Feast: Thirty-First Sunday in Ordinary Time (C)
Suggested Music: *Bamboo Waterfall* **or "We Believe in**
You"/*Gentle Sounds*

It is impossible to judge a person fairly if you don't have all the facts. And yet, we as a people continually make decisions based on religions, politics, dress, and social status. Does these factors really give us a clear picture of a person? Probably not. In this day and age where do you think you might find Jesus? Is he going to be driving a convertible BMW down the freeway? What do you think?

It is most likely safe to say that we would find Jesus in places and with people whom *we* would not choose to be seen with. Why would Jesus make these choices? Jesus made the same choices two thousand years ago, much to the dismay of his followers. The Jews thought that if there was a glaring sinner it would be either be a prostitute or a tax collector. Tax collectors, sometimes called publicans, were the lowest of the low, often collecting too much tax from the poor to give to the Roman government or to pocket the difference. Bribes and stealing went hand in hand with being a tax collector. And yet Jesus accepted the friendship of a funny little man called Zacchaeus, the chief tax collector.

Release your imagination, joining Jesus when he first meets Zacchaeus.

Meditation

Move into a comfortable position....Move your shoulders....
Close your eyes....Take a deep breath....Let it out slowly....
Whisper, "Jesus."....Look into the mirror of life....The
reflection is you....

You are approaching the gates of the city of Jericho.... Jesus,
placing a hand on your arm, guides you through the throngs
of people....The disciples are busy talking among
themselves....Jesus turns toward you and smiles. "I like this
part of the day."....Jesus points toward the setting sun....The
sky is filled with puffs of orange-streaked clouds....The blue
sky of day peeks through the haze of color, holding onto the
sunlight as long as possible....

Soon, a crowd begins to gather around Jesus....You are lost in
the pressing sea of people....You have lost track of Jesus....
The disciple, Andrew, tries to grab your hand but is shoved
aside....You hear a man yelling, "Let me through! I must see
Jesus."....At last, Andrew makes his way to your side, clearing
a path for you toward Jesus....A strange little man pushes
through yelling, "I can't see Jesus!"....His short, stubby, little
legs propel his stocky body up and down, straining for a
glimpse of Jesus....John, being much taller, holds the crowd in
check to allow the man through the sea of legs....Instead of
waiting patiently, he shoves and pushes his way to a tall
sycamore tree....Grasping the limbs of the tree, he pulls
himself up into the branches, perching on a bough high above
the street...."That man is a rich tax collector. The people hate
him. That's why they didn't let him through to see Jesus,"
James explains....James pushes through the milling crowd to
Jesus' side....Jesus glances your way, "Are you getting walked
on?" he asks....

Jesus stops under the bent sycamore tree, first noting all the
people, then glancing up and noticing Zacchaeus....Partially
annoyed, partially surprised, Jesus snaps, "Zacchaeus, come
down out of the tree right now! I will be staying at your house
tonight."....A hiss sounds through the throng.... Clearly this is

not a popular decision....Peter places his hand on Jesus' shoulder, "Don't talk to that man; he is a sinner....Surely, you don't mean that you are really going to go to his house, a house bought with bribes!"....Before Jesus can respond, Zacchaeus climbs down the tree....The stunted little man stands no taller than your waist. His mouth falls open as Jesus takes Zacchaeus' hand in his.... His clothing is covered with tree bark and pitch....Leaves stick to his beard like velcro.... His right foot is bare, his toes twitching through a hole in his sock....The seat of his pants are ripped, showing much too much of his red underwear....You begin to giggle at the sight....The corners of Jesus' mouth twitch, inviting a grin.... Zacchaeus looks up at Jesus. "I know that I have done some really bad things in my life, but now I want to make up for it. I will give half of all I have to the poor. And if I ever cheated anyone out of money, I will pay him back four times as much."....Jesus places his arm around Zacchaeus' shoulder as they walk toward Zacchaeus' home....Peter, not to be outdone, calls out, "You're going to be sorry, Jesus. Just remember I told you so!"....Andrew whispers, "Pete just always wants the last word. Are you ever like that?" he asks. (*Pause.*) The stub of a man talks a mile a minute....Jesus occasionally nods his head. Through a grove of trees you catch glimpses of the largest house you have ever seen.

Zacchaeus invites everyone into his home....Beautiful gardens surround the large pink house....Zacchaeus's chubby body shakes like Jell-O as he rushes about making plans for his guests....His excitement fills the house...."Me! My house! I can't believe he would eat dinner with me!" he exclaims...."I can't believe it either," Peter grumbles....Look around at all the riches, the house, jewelry, servants, gardens, pools.... Catching up with Zacchaeus, you ask, "How can you give all this up?"....Zacchaeus stops momentarily, "I have been touched by God. I will find new life in following the man Jesus."....Once again, he hurries off to the kitchen.

Jesus, knowing the questions on your heart, takes you by the arm....You and Jesus walk toward the garden...."I know what you are thinking. Zacchaeus will be less concerned about his own life and more concerned with others," Jesus says softly. Picking a blossom from the bush, he hands you the fragrant bloom. "Once I knew that Zacchaeus was willing to make changes in his life I was willing to wipe his slate clean. He has a new chance in life; his sins are forgiven....Are you willing to make some changes? Regardless of the past, your future can be with me."....Jesus is waiting patiently for your answer.

Take this time to be alone with Jesus. Look into your heart.

Prayer

Jesus, I could be found up many trees in my life. I accept your love and forgiveness. May I find the strength to change as Zacchaeus did. Thank you for your friendship. Amen.

It is time to leave Jesus in the garden. Say goodbye....Walk through the garden gate....Down the path....Open your eyes and return to this room.

Discussion

- Why do you think Zacchaeus wanted to see Jesus? (*Point out that it may have just been curiosity at first.*)

- What would Jesus say to you if he found you up a tree?

- What is the important lesson here? (*We can always start over by making changes in our lifestyle. God is forgiving.*)

Closing

Prior to class, using small rounded river stones, use a marker to write on the stones: "peace," "love," "charity," "forgiveness," "strength," "wisdom," "honesty," and "faith." Make several stones of each word. Pass around a basket of the stones, inviting students to select one that most clearly symbolizes a gift they could use right now.

Optional: Share with others in your group the gift you choose and why.

Close with a group Our Father.

Sing several verses of "Kum Ba Yah," adding, "Someone is forgiven, Lord."

■ Music Resources

Background music for guided meditations is readily available from both religious and secular stores. Listen for music that can set a mood, usually peaceful, but does not call attention to itself. In working with teens, I have found that using a background of nature sounds combined with music is the most effective choice. This type of music provides a relaxing environment, not causing the teen to "turn off" with an improper music selection. Here are some of my favorites.

Arkenstone, David. *Another Star in the Sky*. Narada Music.

Bamboo Waterfall. Northwood Music (1-800-336-6398 for dealer). A combination of music and nature sounds, wind chimes, bells, waterfalls, wind, waves, and streams.

Darnell, Dik. *Ceremony*. Etherean Music. Beautiful instrumentals that work well with the meditations.

In the Spirit We Belong. Canadian Conference of Catholic Bishops.

Landry, Carey. *Gentle Sounds*. OCP. This album works well with the meditations. The music is arranged so that you are able to cross from one piece to the next without disrupting the meditation.

Fitzgerald, Scott. *Dreamland*. Northwood Music. Gentle music blends calming sounds of waves, rain, crickets, and other nature sounds.

Haugen, Marty. *Instruments of Peace*. GIA. You may need to be more selective about music choice for each meditation.

Richard, Gary. *Dream Journey*. Northwood Music. Blends soft, dreamy music with soothing natural sounds. Cassette #M41C, CD #M41D.

———. *Water Music*. Northwood Music. Guitar plus nature's most eloquent instrument, water.

Sea, The. Northwood Music. Waves on sandy beaches, crashing waves, tide pools, seagulls, other sounds of nature. Effective and relaxing.

Thunderstorms. Northwood Music. The rush of wind, rolling thunder, heavy rainfall, very dramatic.

Winston, George. *December*. Windham Hill Productions.

Index of Meditations According to Cycles

Cycle A

Advent & Christmas

Lent, Triduum, & Easter

Ordinary Time

Cycle B

Advent & Christmas

Lent, Triduum, & Easter

Ordinary Time

Cycle C

Advent & Christmas

Lent, Triduum, & Easter

Index of Meditations According to Cycles

Ordinary Time

Catechesis & Fatih Sharing

EUCHARIST
An Eight-Session Ritual-Catechesis Experience for Adults

Susan S. Jorgensen

Paper, 200 pages, 8½" x 11", ISBN: 0-89390-293-4

Participants in this eight-week program work through the prayers of the Eucharistic liturgy, from opening rite to dismissal, and emerge with deep understanding of the words and gestures of the Eucharist.

CATECHIZING WITH LITURGICAL SYMBOLS
25 Hands-on Sessions for Teens and Adults

Pamela J. Edwards

Paper, 128 pages, 8½" x 11", ISBN: 0-89390-401-5

These 25 liturgical symbols will touch you. You know the power of symbols. The power to inspire. To enrich. To deepen faith. But most resources on symbols are dry, wordy, theoretical treatises. Not this one. *Catechizing with Liturgical Symbols* is a practical, 25-session program for expanding family understanding and sensitivity for symbols. In these sessions, people interact with these symbols, are touched by them, and let them become a part of their faith experience. Creating symbols can also be used as therapeutic exercises that promote healing. The examples included in this work can be done at home, in the classroom or with a worship environment, all with a minimum of aesthetic training and only a small investment in time or money.

A BOOK OF RITUAL PRAYERS
30 Celebrations for Parishes, Schools, and Faith Communities

Jerry Welte and Marlene Kemper Welte

Paper, 160 pages, 5½" x 8½", ISBN: 0-89390-397-3

Vatican II called for a liturgical renewal that puts participation as "the aim to be considered before all else." These 30 celebrations are intended to celebrate the community's faith through an emphasis on basic Christian symbols. These celebrations will help you rediscover the long-standing tradition of a rich liturgical life with a variety of rituals and devotions for the various seasons, feasts and events which mark a journey of faith. This resource is perfect for any community that seeks out creative ways to celebrate God's presence.

Story & Drama

THREE-MINUTE DRAMAS FOR WORSHIP

Karen Patitucci

Paper, 261 pages, 5½" x 8½", ISBN: 0-89390-143-1

Here are 72 easy-to-memorize skits perfect for your church, classroom, or prayer group. The Bible-based dramas include theme and Scripture references that will help you decide which ones best fit your particular needs. Also includes tips on how to write and direct your own short dramas.

CREATIVE STORYTELLING

Marsh Cassady, PhD

Three Audio Cassettes

These audio cassettes are adapted from the author's books *Storytelling Step-By-Step* and *Creating Stories for Storytelling*. Learn all the steps to successful storytelling: selecting the right story for your audience, adapting your story for different occasions and audiences, analyzing it, preparing your audience, and presenting the story. You'll also find ideas for creating your own original stories, plotting a story, creating tension, and writing dialogue that will keep your listeners on the edge of their chairs. The author's theatrical experience helps the example stories take on a life of their own.

CRUSHED INTO GLORY
And Other Dramas for Preaching and Teaching

Joseph J. Juknialis and James Heimerl

Paper, 224 pages, 6" x 9", ISBN: 0-89390-340-X

Eighteen lectionary-based dramas that put the Word of God into a contemporary context. There are several dramas for each season and cycle of the church year. They are ready to help you tweak the imagination of people in your congregation. Use them as an occasional alternative to traditional preaching, in class, or with youth groups.

Youth Ministry

YOUTH MINISTRY ACTIVITY BOOK
For Ages 11-14

Rose Thomas Stupak, I.H.M.

Paper, 105 pages, 5½" x 8½", ISBN: 0-89390-127-X

"The author offers a cafeteria of ideas that you can build on, according to your own situation. She provides you with the basic ingredients to structure your own pilgrimage, retreat, service project, dramatization, song, and pantomime for your specific group of teens."
— Liguorian Magazine.

YOUR WILL BE DONE ON EARTH
Eco-Spirituality Activities for 12-15 Year Olds

Christie L. Jenkins, PhD

Paper, Eighteen lesson plans,
120 pages, 8½" x 11", ISBN: 0-89390-254-3

"An excellent book for teaching adolescents about environmental issues from a religious, theological, and scientific perspective."
— Theological Book Service

ACTING IT OUT
74 Short Plays for Starting Discussions with Teenagers

Joan Sturkie & Marsh Cassady, Ph.D.

Paper, 358 pages, 6" x 9", ISBN: 0-89390-178-4

Use these 74 short dramas with teenagers to explore the serious problems that affect their lives, from anorexia to sexual abuse to suicide. Discussion questions at the end of each drama. Ideal for classes in peer helping or for high school classes, and youth.

Youth Ministry

THE SEVEN PRINCIPLES OF EFFECTIVE YOUTH MINISTRY
Mark Springer and Cheryl Smith

Paper, 192 pages, 5½" x 8½", ISBN: 0-89390-341-8

"Up to date without being trendy, God-centered without being impossible, the authors are offering us something that is both information and inspiration... this book will feed the passion."
— Richard Rohr, OFM Center for Action and Contemplation.

CULTIVATING CHARACTER
Parent-Teacher Resources
for Grades 9, 10, 11, and 12
Richard H. Buchholz

Stapled, illustrated, photocopiable pages,
32 pages, 8½" x 11"
ISBN: 0-89390-407-4 (Grade 9), ISBN: 0-89390-406-6 (Grade 10)
ISBN: 0-89390-405-8 (Grade 11), ISBN: 0-89390-404-X (Grade 12)

With these *Cultivating Character* resource books, you use proven principles to prepare young people to become good parents, workers, and citizens. Each book contains a "thought for the month" master, along with background information, that can be photocopied and posted on bulletin boards, given to students for hanging in lockers or keeping with their personal journals, and mailed to parents for posting on refrigerator doors. Simple. Easy. And effective.

STAY IN SCHOOL, STAY OUT OF PRISON
David Stuart Schofield #334387

Paper, 80 pages, 8" x 8", ISBN: 0-89390-366-3
Pen-and-ink illustrations

Give young people a view of prison life almost as intense as being there. *Stay in School, Stay out of Prison* is an illustrated book by an insider — a lifer in a maximum security prison. It covers the many freedoms lost when one is in prison, the living situation, death row and forms of execution, food, the danger of prison life, and much more. The haunting pen-and-ink drawings make this a "Scared Straight" program in a book.

Catechist Training

COME TO THE WEDDING FEAST:
An Eight-Session Course for Training Catechists

Dominic F. Ashkar, PhD

Paper, 96 pages, 8½" x 11", ISBN: 0-89390-400-7

This eight-session program helps Directors of Religious Education to lead their catechists into becoming more spiritually effective. Using the text of the Wedding at Cana as a base, this guidebook serves as an invitation to a journey that connects your catechists with Jesus and the disciples. Each session includes handouts with permission to photo-copy.

RCIA SPIRITUALITY
Formation for the
Catechumenate Team

Barbara Hixon with Reflection Questions by Gael Gensler, OSF

Paper, 192 pages, 5½" x 8½", ISBN: 0-89390-399-X

Barbara Hixon and Gael Gensler have a straightforward message: the catechumenal process is not something you do to someone else. It's something that happens to you, the team member, as much as to the catechumen. They show you how each step of the catechumenate process will change your life. Gael Gensler's questions help turn this book, a revision of the original RCIA Ministry, into a useful group formation tool for your team.

Order from your local bookseller, or contact:

Resource Publications, Inc.
160 E. Virginia Street #290
San Jose, CA 95112-5876
1-408-286-8505 (questions)
1-408-287-8748 (fax)
1-888-273-7782 (orders, toll-free)

LQ